PRAGMATIC DATA ANALYSIS

Pragmatic Data Analysis

R. VERYARD

MA, MSc
Data Logic Ltd,
London

BLACKWELL SCIENTIFIC PUBLICATIONS

OXFORD LONDON EDINBURGH

BOSTON PALO ALTO MELBOURNE

© 1984 by
Blackwell Scientific Publications
Editorial offices:
Osney Mead, Oxford, OX2 0EL
8 John Street, London, WC1N 2ES
9 Forrest Road, Edinburgh, EH1 2QH
52 Beacon Street, Boston
   Massachusetts 02108, USA
706 Cowper Street, Palo Alto
   California 94301, USA
99 Barry Street, Carlton
   Victoria 3053, Australia

First published 1984

Phototypesetting by
Parkway Illustrated Press, Abingdon.
Printed and bound in Great Britain

Distributed in North America by
Computer Science Press Inc.,
11 Taff Court,
Box 6030, Rockville,
Maryland 20850, USA

British Library
Cataloguing in Publication Data

Veryard, R.
   Pragmatic data analysis
   1. Mathematic statistics—Data processing
   I. Title
   519.4   QA276.4

ISBN 0-632-01311-7

Contents

Preface

It is customary etiquette at this point for the author to modestly acknowledge the imperfections of the book (without being honest enough to admit what they are) and to express gratitude to a selection of friends and acquaintances who helped create the book. It is usually felt necessary to stress — although it should go without saying — that there is no connection between the faults and the friends.

As I see it, the main fault in the book is the inadequate division between description and prescription. I have neither given an objective and uninterpreted account of the methods employed in a typical DP department, nor have I started from first principles and the latest research in order to develop a brand new formulation of my own, which would be wholly logically sound and sophisticated. I have presented a mixture of prescription and description. It follows that the methods outlined in this book cannot be adopted uncritically, but the reader is obliged to think how best to adapt them to his own needs. He must work out himself how to bridge some of the gaps. I had not realized when I started writing just how many gaps there would have to be, which I could only fill by embarking on a completely different course than I had originally planned. It is probably impossible in this subject to be both comprehensible and comprehensive.

My gratitude goes to the following:

to anyone who may have had these ideas before me. I am not always able to remember where I read or heard these ideas, but I am certainly not clever enough to think it all up by myself — my apologies for any unwitting plagiarism;

to Ian Palmer, for whom I once worked, whose formation was a stimulus and starting point for my own thinking;

to those who have worked with me on data analysis exercises, especially Raimo Rikkilae, Francis Murphy, Angela Simonsson and Kevin Swindells — the best way of learning is to discuss with a colleague;

to those whom I have attempted to teach, whose incomprehension and questions have forced me to find new expressions and problems;

to my secretary, Sarah Starr, for managing the text;

to my employer, Data Logic, for encouraging and assisting me to go into print;

to the estate of the late Sonia Brownell Orwell and Martin Secker & Warburg Ltd for permission to quote from George Orwell's *Collected Essays, Journalism and Letters* (1931).

Chapter 1

Introduction

Introduction

This chapter introduces the notion of data analysis and explains its importance. The book as a whole rests on three premises, which are outlined below.

First, that information is an important asset or resource. For any information system, whether or not computerized, and particularly where data are shared between subsystems (i.e. almost always), a clear and accurate knowledge of the data structure is needed.

Second, that data analysis is a branch of systems analysis and therefore shares its principles. Of particular relevance are the separation of analysis from design, the clear statement of objectives, assumptions and priorities, the systematic top–down and iterative approaches to analysis, and the unambiguous documentation of results.

Third, that data analysis is not (at least not yet) a fully mechanical activity. The data analyst often has to make arbitrary decisions on a criterion of elegance, or according to what the users are likely to understand and agree with. This book gives guidelines to common sense; its procedures are no substitute for intelligence.

Data analysis

What is data analysis? As its name implies, it is a branch of systems analysis concerned with the structure of data within a system. Whereas the techniques of systems analysis were first worked out by military advisors for the design of weapons systems, data analysis is special to the data processing (DP) industry. Since the structure and flow of data is of central importance in any DP system, data analysis is central to any DP systems analysis. In the past, data analysis was often carried out implicitly, unrecognized. Ad hoc techniques, based on common sense and experience, were used to translate the users' data requirements into file types and record types. Nowadays, as DP systems grow more complex, and with the increasing use of large databases, these ad hoc methods are being replaced by more formal methodologies. The results

1

of the analysis are documented in a standard format, often using an automated data dictionary. Checks for logical consistency between subsystems can be carried out easily, and any file or database design proceeds smoothly, because the data requirements are unambiguously and clearly defined.

   In particular, the following advantages of data analysis are generally recognized within commercial data processing departments.

1 The users' requirements of data structure tend to be much more stable than their functional requirements. This means that a computer systems design based on a proper analysis of the data structure is less likely to need extensive modification whenever the business needs change, than one based on current operations and functions. Maintenance of badly designed and inflexible computer systems is a serious problem in most large computer installations.

2 The results of the data analysis are in a form that can easily be understood by the users themselves. Discussion of their requirements, including negotiation between conflicting user departments, can be based on a clear statement of the data structure. This is obviously better than producing a computerese system specification, in which the user cannot hope to find the flaws. Systems developed from such documents rarely provide user satisfaction.

Data modelling

A data model of an organization is a systematic representation of the data requirements of the organization. Such a model is independent of any computerized or manually operated system; however, any system design should be based on such a model. The model documents the structure of and the interrelationships between the data. The differing requirements of the different departments and of the different functional areas of the organization are contained and reconciled in the model. The model is presented as a combination of simple diagrams and written definitions.

Data and information

It will come as no surprise to the reader of a data processing textbook to be told of the importance of data. In order to demonstrate this importance, let us compare a commercial organization with the human body.

Human anatomy includes a system to circulate oxygen and nutrients to all parts of the body, carried by the bloodstream and pumped by the heart. This corresponds to the circulation of goods, services and cash in a commercial organization. There is also a system to monitor the operations of the body, to issue instructions to the limbs and vital organs, and to gather information from the outside world via the sense organs. Messages are passed along special channels, i.e. nerves. This corresponds to the flow of data in a commercial organization.

Decisions are made in the brain on the basis of available information. This information is provided by the nervous system and either used immediately or stored for future use. This corresponds to the supply of information to the managers of a commercial organization for the purposes of decision-making.

Finally, let us consider what happens to a part of the human body when the nerve connections are broken. This usually results in paralysis, and if the paralysed part is a vital organ then the body will soon die. This corresponds to a major loss of data within an organization, such as might be caused by the computer catching fire. It may surprise the reader to learn that a serious fire in the computer room is more likely to cause bankruptcy than a serious fire in the warehouse. In other words, the loss of data may be more disastrous than the loss of goods. Therefore data may be more valuable than goods.

The value of data depends on six aspects.

1 *Accurate.* The data must enable correct decisions to be taken. However, unnecessary precision should be avoided. Detailed accounts may be accurate to the nearest penny, but the national budget may be accurate only to the nearest million pounds; further accuracy would be pointless.

2 *Prompt.* The data must be sufficiently up-to-date to allow prompt action to be taken. Often it is the first person to obtain information who gains the commercial benefit. The wealth of the Rothschild family is at least partly due to the intelligence of Nathan Rothschild, who was the first person in London to learn the result of the battle of Waterloo. He had set up a network of spies to bring him the news, and he had time to make many successful speculative deals before the news became public.

3 *Well directed.* The data must be available to the appropriate person within the organization. This has a positive aspect (the right person gets the information he needs) and a negative aspect (the wrong person does not have access to confidential or private data).

4 *Brief.* The important data should not be submerged in a mass of non-essential details, which may lead vital items to be overlooked.

5 *Rare*. The value of any piece of information depends on its unlike-liness or unexpectedness.

6 *Complete*. A list of items will usually be assumed complete, unless the contrary is made clear. An item being incorrectly omitted may be as dangerous as an item being incorrectly included. In some circumstances, however, selective lists are acceptable.

Finally in this section we should state the relationship between data and information. There is no formal distinction between the two; for the purposes of this book, *information* is that which is used for decision-making, *data* are the messages that are passed and stored within an organization. In other words, data are transformed into information by being interpreted and used by a decision-maker. Data plus interpretation equals information.

Shared data

The importance of data stems from their use in communication. Data are communicated in two dimensions: in time, i.e. from the past to the future, and in space, i.e. from one part of the organization to another. Both of these aspects of data must be understood by the analyst. Communication in time requires the concept of data storage; communication in space requires the concept of data sharing.

Why should data be shared at all? If two areas require the same or similar information, the alternative to sharing is copying; but if several copies of the information are maintained independently, this leads to inefficiency and inconsistency. Sharing data means that all user areas are provided with the same, equally up-to-date information.

The data analyst is therefore obliged to examine each item of data that is common to several user areas and ensure that the assumptions made about these data in these different areas do not conflict.

Systems and system objectives

Systems are not restricted to computer software, and the analysis of a clerical system with the aim of computerizing some of it should not limit itself to analysing the parts that are destined for automation. The scope of an analysis should always be broader than that of any subsequent design. A system exists to carry out some *function* of the organization in which it resides; the carrying-out of the function does not end when the computer displays or prints the result of some calculation, it does not end until some human being has taken the result and used it to some purpose. A good system involves the co-operation of man and computer; a good analyst must understand the human side of the system as well as the machine side.

A decision may be made by a human expert on the basis of intuitive judgement and 'feel'. It might be impossible or prohibitively expensive (or politically inconvenient or morally unacceptable) to program a computer to make that decision. But the system as a whole needs that decision made in order to carry out the function for which it is designed. A description of the system would be incomplete without mentioning the need for human intervention.

The objectives of a system should be expressed in terms of the function of the system for the organization and not in terms of the role of the computer specifically. Words like 'facilitate' usually imply the latter.

The objective of a stock control system is 'to avoid excess stock building up, without running out of anything'. It is *not* 'to provide regular management reports facilitating prompt decisions on stock levels'. The computer may do the latter, the system does the former. In evaluating the system, the contribution of any computer should be considered, but always in terms of the objectives of the whole system.

No methodology solves all problems

A few warning words about methodologies in general, and data analysis in particular. There is an ancient Chinese proverb: 'A legless man cannot walk on stilts.' No methodology can be a substitute for common-sense and experience, it can only supplement these. If a methodology gives you checklists or questionnaires, use them — but use your brain too! Data analysts are often given forms to fill in, to aid the documentation of each entity, relationship and attribute. It is a mistake to suppose that filling in such a form always exhausts the information that should be recorded. No standard form, no methodology can be that flexible.

This book is compatible with most commonly used methodologies, in that they all call for some kind of data analysis, and for the production of a data model. The format of the data model itself may vary, but the concepts are usually the same. When working within a particular methodology, there may be additional procedures to follow, documentation to be produced in a different way, or even a different notation to learn. However, if the reader has grasped the essential concepts introduced in this book, their adaption to new problem areas, within the guidelines of a particular methodology or a set of formal standards, should not cause any difficulties.

Furthermore, a good analyst does not restrict himself to the form of data modelling he has been taught, but is prepared to use different constructs and techniques — of his own invention where necessary — if the nature of the problem requires it. The models described in this book have been proved adequate over a very wide range of problems, but are by no means universally applicable.

Chapter 2

Data Modelling Concepts

Introduction

The objective of analysing the data structure of a particular information system is to express this structure in the form of a *data model*. In a data model, the information is represented by a small number of different constructs. In this chapter, the most widely used form of data model will be described.

There are two philosophical attitudes towards data modelling, known respectively as *semantic relativism* and *semantic absolutism*. According to the absolutist way of thinking, there is only one correct or ideal way of modelling anything; each object in the real world must be represented by a particular construct. Semantic relativists, on the other hand, believe that most things in the real world can be modelled in many different ways, using any of the basic constructs. Marriage, for example may be represented in the model by an entity, a relationship, an attribute, a function, a domain, a constraint, a role, or in a number of other ways. Depending on the circumstances, some of these ways may be more useful, or may result in a more elegant model, but none is uniquely correct. This book adopts a relatavist standpoint.

The philosophical difference does not have to cause any practical problems when semantic relativists work alongside semantic absolutists. The absolutist's quest for the ideal model need not conflict with the relativist's quest for the best model.

Many different modelling schemes have been proposed, offering different sets of constructs from which the models can be built. The basic constructs may include any of those mentioned in the context of the marriage . example above. For the purpose of this book, the constructs that will be used to build the data models are *entities, relationships* between entities, and *attributes* of entities.

Having decided how to represent the information in the real world with a set of entities, relationships and attributes, each entity, each relationship and each attribute must be named and precisely defined. Additional information (for example, statistical data) may be recorded where available. Sometimes a picture of the model, known as an *entity-relationship* (E-R) *diagram*, is drawn, showing the entities as boxes and the relationships as lines connecting the boxes; such a diagram gives a useful overview but cannot replace the definitions.

What is an entity?

An *entity* is any object of interest to the organization under investigation, any part of the system, any object about which data can be collected and stored. An entity can be real or conceptual; an activity, a passing state or a grouping can be an entity.

A data analysis for an insurance company might describe the business in terms of the following entities:

> policyholders
> brokers
> accidents
> policies
> claims
> payments
> vehicles
> risks

A vehicle is a real object, a broker is a person, an accident is an event, a policy is a written agreement, and a risk is an abstract classification. All of these may be entities.

In this chapter, I shall use as my main example of an organization a sports authority. Cricket fans may like to think of the Test and County Cricket Board; soccer supporters could think of the F.A.; American readers may prefer the National Football League. The entities of interest to the authority could well include the following:

> players
> clubs
> teams
> managers
> matches
> results of matches
> trophies
> playing grounds

Exercise 1
List some probable entities for a clearing bank, for an airline, for a local education authority, for the Ministry of Defence.

Entity occurrences and entity types

It is sometimes necessary to distinguish between entities as individuals on the one hand and entities as classifications of individuals on the other. Where confusion would otherwise arise, it is common to speak of *occurrences* for the former entities and *types* for the latter. From our sports example: Old Trafford is an *entity occurrence* which belongs to the *entity type* GROUND.

Exercise 2
Name some occurrences of the entity types PLAYER, CLUB. To which types do the following entities (i.e. entity occurrences) belong: Middlesex, Ian Botham, Washington Redskins, Lords, Kevin Keegan, Super Bowl, Spurs, Cup Final, Roger Staubach.

Relationships

Although the basic component of the data model is the entity, the data model is not merely a collection of entities. The model must be given a structure, which we define in terms of the relationships between entities. Loosely speaking, two entity occurrences are related if the removal of one makes a significant difference to the other. For example, when a married man dies, his wife becomes a widow. If such a connection between two entity occurrences can be generalized and named, so that it can be applied to several similar situations, that is then a *relationship*. For example, the relationship between married women and their husbands is called *marriage*.

Relationships may be permanent and unchangeable, or they may be temporary or transient, only lasting for a short while. For example, the relationship between a buyer and a seller only lasts as long as the sale itself. There are also semi-permanent relationships, such as that between an employer and an employee.

Some of the classes of relationship that can be included in the data model are

logical & causal	e.g.	*is necessary for*
		is controller of
inclusion & membership	e.g.	*is part of*
		belongs to
personal & contractual	e.g.	*is supplier of*
		is manager of

Just as the names of entities tend to be nouns, relationships tend to be referred to by verbs or verbal phrases. However, the reader will find many examples of relationships, in this book and elsewhere, that do not follow this rule.

Any two entity types may have a relationship defined between them. The *degree* of a relationship is based on the number of occurrences of the entity types that can be related to one another. The possible degrees are *one-to-one, one-to-many* (or *many-to-one*) and *many-to-many*.

A relationship is called *one-to-one* if each occurrence of the first entity type is related to only one occurrence of the second entity type and each occurrence of the second related to only one of the first.

Example: each match has just one result and each result refers to only one match. Therefore the relationship between MATCH and MATCH RESULT is one-to-one.

A relationship is called *one-to-many* if an occurrence of the first entity type may be related to several occurrences of the second, but each occurrence of the second is related to only one occurrence of the first. A relationship is called *many-to-one* if each occurrence of the first entity type is related to only one occurrence of the second, but an occurrence of the second may be related to several occurrences of the first. A many-to-one relationship is clearly a one-to-many relationship viewed the opposite way around.

Example: a player may only be a member of one club (at any one time), but a club (obviously) has many players as members. Therefore the relationship *is member of* between the entity type PLAYER and the type CLUB is many-to-one.

A relationship is called *many-to-many* if an occurrence of the first entity type may be related to several occurrences of the second, and vice versa.

Example: a player plays in several matches, a match has several (i.e. 22) players playing in it. Therefore the relationship *plays in* between PLAYER and MATCH is many-to-many.

A relationship may be *involuted,* i.e. relate occurrences of one entity type to other occurrences of the same type. For example, a sub-lieutenant can be promoted to lieutenant but not (directly) to lieutenant commander. This can be shown as an involuted relationship from the entity type RANK to itself. It is many-to-many relationship because there is more then one promotion path from rating to admiral.

Exercise 3

What are the other relationships between the entity types in our sports example? How should these relationships be classified? Which of them are one-to-one, many-to-one, many-to-many?

Attributes

An entity is defined as an object about which data can be stored. These data are classified as attributes. Each entity type can have a number of attributes associated with it. Each occurrence of that entity type may then have a value for each attribute.

For example, the entity type PLAYER may have the attributes *name, preferred position, nationality,* etc. An individual player, who is an occurrence of the type PLAYER, will have values for these attributes, for example:

name:	Alan Knott
position:	Wicket-keeper
nationality:	British

For each entity, a number of relevant attributes can usually be listed. Consider the entities of our sports example. The attributes of CLUB might include: name, date last won championship, number of overseas players, etc. The attributes of GROUND might include: name, location, capacity, number of parking spaces, whether licensed refreshments, etc.

Exercise 4
For the entities listed in your answer to Exercise 1, suggest a few attributes of each entity that would be of interest to the organization in question. (For possible solutions, see the answer to Exercise 1 in Appendix II.)

Logical constraints

In order to keep the structure of the data model simple and easy to understand, the division between entities, relationships and attributes must be kept quite clear. Relationships can only be defined between entities; attributes can only belong to entities. In particular, the following constructs must be avoided, because they are unnecessary and lead to confusion:

attributes belonging to attributes;
attributes belonging to relationships;
relationships being defined between attributes.

Entity-relationship (E-R) diagrams

In most areas of systems analysis, a pictorial or diagrammatic representation of a structure is much easier to understand than a verbal description. In data analysis, a diagram (sometimes known as a Bachman diagram) may be drawn to show the relationships between the entities.

An entity is represented by a box (Fig. 2.1).

Fig. 2.1

A relationship is represented by a line between two boxes (Fig. 2.2)

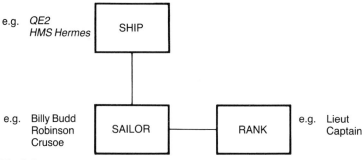

Fig. 2.2

A ship has many sailors, but a sailor is on only one ship. A sailor has one rank, many sailors have the same rank. Therefore both these relationships are many-to-one. The involuted relationship on RANK is many-to-many. This is all shown on the diagram using crows-feet. A many-to-many relationship has crows-feet at both ends and a one-to-one relationship has no crows-feet. A many-to-one relationship has a crows-foot at the 'many' end. See the navy model in Fig. 2.3.

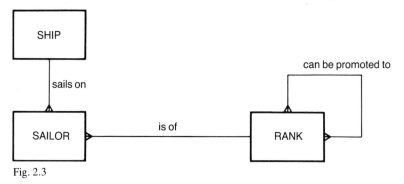

Fig. 2.3

Exercise 5

Draw an E-R diagram for a sports authority. (For suggested solution see Appendix II.)

Chapter 3

How to Produce a Data Model

Introduction

The data requirements of the user are to be analysed, and the data structure is to be modelled in terms of entities, attributes and relationships: that is what this book is all about. In this chapter, the techniques of analysis will be described. The approach is an iterative one. Initial discussions with the user, or analysis of written system descriptions, will yield a list of possible entities, and the analyst should be able to draw a speculative entity-relationship diagram. This is then used as the basis for further discussion. Successive versions of the model will be more detailed, more accurate, more inclusive and more precisely defined, until all concerned are satisfied with the model.

Approach and attack

The approach of the data analyst will depend partly on the nature of the system he is investigating. An operational system presents somewhat different problems from an information system. An *operational* system is one concerned with the day-to-day running of the organization (e.g. sales order processing); an *information* system is one concerned with providing statistical or summarized information for managers, shareholders, and other decision makers. Often, a whole system is a hybrid, containing both operational and information subsystems.

An operational system is considerably easier to analyse than an information system. Whereas an operational system must carry out certain definite functions, which can be observed in the current paperwork, the function of an information system is to provide 'useful' information, with no clear criterion of usefulness. (We may ignore the special case of company reports, where certain accounting data have to be present. However, most company reports contain more information than the legal minimum.)

Consider a 'pure' information system, i.e. one with no operational features. The system collects raw data from various sources, collates and summarizes them and outputs statistical information.

14

There are four different points of attack for the analyst:

1   the raw data presently available;
2   the raw data potentially or conceivably available;
3   the results required (i.e. specifically demanded by the users of the system);
4   the results potentially required (i.e. identified by the analyst as being valuable for the decisions which have to be taken).

The analyst should not limit himself to one of these points of attack. Although the output is more important than the input, the input structure should not be ignored. The information that may be required ad hoc cannot be fully predicted. Any additional raw data that can be included at comparatively low cost (e.g. extra items on a tape that must be read anyway) should be considered. A computerized information system must allow the user to obtain any conceivable, statistically summarized combination of the available data.

If in doubt whether to include something in your data model, because you do not know whether the information would in fact be useful or not, it is better to include it. When the model is complete and verified, then each item of marginal relevance can be subjected to a cost/benefit analysis to see whether it is worth recording. (But when your time is limited, do not spend too long on such marginal items.)

The style of data analysis described in this book is strictly non-hierarchical. Students familiar with other approaches to analysis sometimes find this a difficulty. When asked to produce a data model of an airline, they start by drawing a box and labelling it airline. This is a mistake. The airline is, in a manner of speaking, the whole thing, not a single entity. Furthermore, unless the airline is storing data about its competitors, there is only one airline in the system: entity types usually have many occurrences.

Remember that an entity is an object about which data can be collected and stored. Find the entities first, look for the relationships afterwards. Do not expect the model of a real-world situation to be a hierarchy.

Finding entity types

Obtain a verbal description of the activities carried out within the area to be analysed. Make a list of all the nouns that occur in this description. For each noun, ask whether it refers to an object — real or conceptual — about which the organization might store information. This list will serve as the starting point for the entity-relationship data model.

The following example may prove instructive. It is a description of hop-picking, taken from George Orwell's *Collected Essays, Journalism and Letters* (1931).

> As to what one can earn, the system of payment is this. Two or three times a day the hops are measured, and you are due a certain sum (in our case twopence) for each bushel you have picked. A good vine yields about half a bushel of hops, and a good picker can strip a vine in about ten minutes, so that theoretically one *might* earn about 30/– by a sixty-hour week. But in practice this is quite impossible. To begin with, the hops vary enormously. On some vines they are as large as small pears, and on others hardly bigger than peas; the bad vines take rather longer to strip than the good ones – they are generally more tangled — and sometimes it needs five or six of them to make a bushel. Then there are all kinds of delays, and the pickers get no compensation for lost time. Sometimes it rains (if it rains hard the hops get too slippery to pick), and one is always kept waiting when changing from field to field, so that an hour or two is wasted every day. And above all there is the question of measurement. Hops are soft things like sponges, and it is quite easy for the measurer to crush a bushel of them into a quart if he chooses. Some days he merely scoops the hops out, but on other days he has orders from the farmer to 'take them heavy', and then he crams them tight into the basket, so that instead of getting 20 bushels for a full bin one gets only 12 or 14, i.e. a shilling or so less . . . . From the bin the hops are put into 10-bushel pokes which are supposed to weigh a hundredweight and are normally carried by one man. It used to take two men to hoist a full poke when the measurer had been taking them heavy.

The nouns in this description can be divided into the following categories.

1 *Real objects:* field, vine, bin, hop, poke, basket.
2 *People:* picker, measurer, farmer, and (by implication) poke-carrier.
3 *Abstract objects relevant to the system:* work, payment, measurement, compensation, delay.
4 *Abstract objects not relevant to the system:* system, thing, question.
5 *Quantities*

> Time: minute, week, day, hour.
> Money: twopence, shilling.
> Volume: bushel, poke, quart.
> Weight: hundredweight.

6 *Adverbial or adjectival nouns:* in practice, some days.
7 *Similes, etc.:* pear, pea, sponge.

These seven categories do not cover all possible cases, but we can illustrate the commonest.

Firstly, we can ignore categories **4**, **6** and **7**. The concept of relevance to the system is difficult to define, but there should be no doubt about the irrelevance of the nouns assigned to category **4** in the example. If in doubt about a noun, leave it in category **3** for the time being.

A quantity is almost certainly an attribute rather than an entity. Quantity of time is perhaps an attribute of work or of delay; quantity of money an attribute of payment or of compensation; volume an attribute of hop measurement. The nouns belonging to categories **1**, **2** and **3** form our first list of possible entities.

Finding relationships and attributes

Having obtained a list of possible entities, we can examine each one in turn, asking what important properties it has, asking what kinds of information are involved, and asking how it relates to other entities on the list. By these means, the definitions, attributes and relationships for an initial rough data model can be found.

A systematic search for relationships will consider each pair of entity types in turn, and will consider whether any useful, relevant, meaningful relationship can be defined between those two entity types. If there are n possible entity types, then there will be $n \times n$ pairs to examine; of course, involuted relationships from an entity type to itself must also be found.

For each relationship found, the information represented may be direct or indirect. Indirect relationships are redundant and should not be included, unless there is any special reason for including them. (This will be discussed later.)

A systematic search for attributes will consider each entity in turn and produce a list of data about the entity that could conceivably be of interest to the organization.

There are various vocabularies (i.e. sets of terms) the data analyst must deal with. Each user area will have a set of terms; each version of the data model will have a set of terms, which must be entities, attributes or relationships.

Initially, the only terms available to the data analyst are the user terms. At later stages, the user terms can be defined from the terms of the data model, which have been perhaps constructed by the analyst himself.

The analyst should try to take account of all user terms in the model. Therefore in drawing up the first version of the data model, any user term that is not already noted as a possible entity or relationship may be noted as a possible attribute. It should be considered for each such possible attribute, which entity type it can belong to. Is it perhaps an attribute of an entity type it can belong to. Is it perhaps an attribute of an entity not yet found? Is it perhaps not an attribute at all but an entity in its own right?

Using current systems

If there are reasonably well-organized files (computer or otherwise) already in use, it is worth examining these to obtain a preliminary version of the data model. According to this, a record type is listed as a possible entity type, a field is listed as a possible attribute and a cross-reference is listed as a possible relationship. It is extremely unlikely that the final version of the data model will bear much resemblance to this, but this approach gives a useful starting point.

Feature analysis

Many users are able to provide immediate and precise definitions of the data elements required. However, the data analyst will often be confronted with a user who is comparatively inarticulate, or who finds it difficult to answer the questions of the analyst in a useful way. A technique that can sometimes be applied in this situation is described in this section. It resembles a game, and the analyst must be careful to avoid the impression that the user is being made fun of. The technique was originally developed for use in psychotherapy, to allow a psychoanalyst to work out the structure of the patient's beliefs.

The names of any data elements, usually from the list of possible entity types, are written on cards. Three cards are selected at random and presented to the user, who is asked to find the odd one out. Two of the elements share a feature not possessed by the third, which the user is asked to specify. For example, given three cards CLUB, PLAYER and MATCH, the feature named by the user might be that a match only lasts 90 minutes, whereas the other two go on for years.

The user should not be forced to name a feature if nothing occurs to him; on the other hand if he names several features they should all be recorded. The analyst must not be selective at this stage, and should not ignore features because they appear obvious or irrelevant.

This procedure is repeated until the analyst has accumulated a list of features at least as long as the number of cards. The user is taken systematically through the cards and asked, for each card, which of the features apply. These responses are drawn onto a rectangular grid. (The technique is sometimes known as the Repertory Grid test.) For some features, the response will not be a simple Yes/No, but the degree of application can be recorded. For example, the user can be asked for a number between 1 (not at all) and 5 (completely).

When several users are being interviewed, a combined list of features is produced, so that each user is asked to classify the cards according to the same features. Grids are then drawn, one for each interviewee, which are then compared. Differences are investigated and reconciled.

Refining the model (user feedback)

When a rough version of the model has been prepared, based on incomplete knowledge and much guesswork, it must then be subjected to criticism from all sides.

From this, one hopes, a better version will emerge. This is an iterative process: successive improvements in the model being made until a satisfactory version is produced.

Criticism is of two kinds: external (or real or empirical) and internal (or logical or rational). External criticism is discussed in this section; internal criticism is discussed in the next section.

External criticism of the content of the model is based on a comparison of the model with the real-world system being modelled. This can only come from users and experts in the user area. A review of the model therefore usually involves people without specific training or experience in data modelling; this will be handled differently according to their intellectual abilities. For people who do not have the aptitude or, more importantly, the time to grapple with the idea of a data model and the notational conventions, the entity-relationship diagram may be an unwelcome confusion. The analyst must take each element of the model and phrase English-language questions in order to verify the model. However, this is usually unnecessary. Most users can be shown the model itself, or the part that applies to them. Both the diagrams and the written definitions can be discussed, as appropriate. There is actually very little notation to learn, and the users need not be bothered with the conceptual niceties.

This questioning of the user will be supplemented by examining any available paperwork or current computer system. The analyst will be expected to produce evidence for any assumptions that are incorporated into the model.

Further externally derived refinements may follow a detailed functional analysis. The functional requirements can also be described in the form of diagrammatic models. The functional models can be of varying types, but it is usually possible to carry out cross-checks, for example to ensure that the functional models do not refer to data not included in the data model, and that they do not make conflicting assumptions.

Refining the model (logical feedback)

Criticism that is based on the structure of the model, rather than on the real-life system being modelled, can be called *internal*. Because certain structures commonly recur, an experienced data analyst will be able to spot possible imperfections in the model without having studied the system itself. The forms of logical refinement thus produced are described in this section.

The first version of the data model will undoubtably be subject to a number of logical weaknesses. This should not worry anybody. The purpose of the rough initial data model is to be a basis for discussion and iterative refinement. At a later stage in the data analysis, the model can be tidied up to improve its logical structure. At this stage, it is often useful to show the model to colleagues for their comments.

The definitions can be examined for coherence and internal consistency. Unsupported assumptions can be questioned. The fundamental logical criteria of data modelling must be satisfied:

> an attribute cannot itself have attributes;
> an attribute cannot itself have relationships;
> a relationship cannot have attributes.

There are a number of specific ways in which commonly recurring situations can be simplified and refined. These are outlined below.

CHECK A relationship is indirect or redundant, in the sense that the information it represents is contained more directly elsewhere in the model.

ACTION Remove the relationship from the model, but document the fact the relationship is of interest, if it is.

Example
(See Fig. 3.1.) The relationship between country and person clearly duplicates the information represented by the other two relationships, and is therefore redundant.

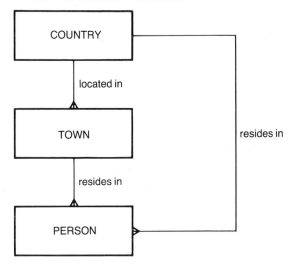

Fig. 3.1

However, care must be taken to avoid removing non-redundant relationships. If, for example, the town of residence is not known for all persons, or if not all persons live in towns, then there will be persons for whom the only way to find out their country of residence is via the direct relationship from person to country, which is therefore in such circumstances not redundant.

CHECK   A many-to-many relationship is included in the model.

ACTION   A many-to-many relationship can usually be resolved by replacing it with a new joining entity and two many-to-one relationships.

Example
(See Fig. 3.2.) In place of a many-to-many relationship between project and employee (one project has many employees working on it, one employee can work on many projects), we now have two many-to-one relationships and an extra entity type.

An employee is assigned to many projects; an employee has many project assignments, each to a single project. We can identify attributes of the new entity, e.g. amount of work done, timespan of involvement on project. The many-to-many relationship between PROJECT and EMPLOYEE is redundant, because the same information is contained via PROJECT ASSIGNMENT.

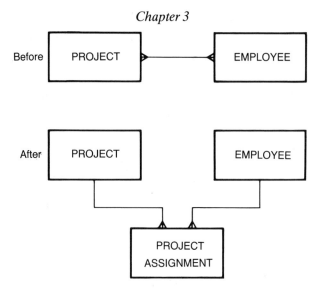

Fig. 3.2

CHECK   A one-to-one relationship is included in the model.

ACTION   Combine the two entity types joined by the relationship into a single entity.

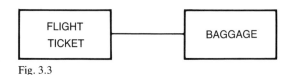

Fig. 3.3

Example

(See Fig. 3.3.) The attributes of BAGGAGE can be included in the FLIGHT TICKET entity. This is because there is no business function that accesses baggage data without accessing the associated flight ticket data.

   The fact that if there were many tickets with no baggage, and if there were many baggage attributes then it might well be implemented as a separate baggage record, is not sufficient reason to separate the entities.

   However, the following is a good example of a one-to-one relationship between two entity types which it would be wrong to combine to a single entity.

   A judge and his caseload are related one-to-one, but we separate the entities for the following reasons: (i) they are conceptually separate; (ii) one judge may take over another's caseload; (iii) caseload data are fast moving, whereas judge data are slow moving; (iv) caseloads are of interest in circumstances where we are not interested in the judges.

CHECK   An attribute is repeated within one entity type. In other words, one entity occurrence can have many values for that attribute at the same time.

ACTION   Remove the attribute from that entity and replace it with a one-to-many or many-to-many relationship to a second (presumably new) entity.

Example

Let us return to our example of a sports authority and consider the attributes of the entity MATCH RESULT in the case of association football. The information that could be collected or stored about this entity might include the following attributes: final score
half-time score
amount of injury time
name of goal scorer
minute in which goal scored

Because several goals can be scored in a single match the last two of these attributes are repeating attributes. In other words, the attribute has several different values for one occurrence of the entity MATCH RESULT. For this reason, these two attributes are not proper attributes of the entity MATCH RESULT but must be attributes of some other entity. In this case, they are obviously attributes of the entity GOAL. We therefore add the entity GOAL to our model; the two attributes, which were repeating attributes when regarded as attributes of the entity MATCH RESULT are not repeating when regarded as attributes of the entity GOAL. There is clearly a one-to-many relationship between the two entities; one match includes many goals, each goal occurs in one match.

CHECK   An entity type is repeated within one attribute. In other words, the entity occurrences fall into groups such that all entities in a single group necessarily have the same value for the attribute.

ACTION   The groups are themselves occurrences of another entity type, perhaps not yet recognized. The attribute is removed to this group entity.

Example

The attribute *colour of shorts* may initially be considered as an attribute of PLAYER. But as all the players of the same team wear the same strip, the attribute should really be regarded as an attribute of TEAM.

It is important to be sure that the groups do not share the attribute values by mere coincidence. For example, when making *salary* an attribute of COMPANY GRADE rather than of EMPLOYEE, it is not enough that all employees at the same grade happen at present to receive the same salary. What matters is that they always do and will. In other words, salary is *functionally dependent* on grade.

CHECK   An attribute belongs to two different entity types. This may be
            disguised: the same attribute may have been given two
            different names.

ACTION   Remove the attribute from one entity and replace it with a
            relationship between the two entities. Alternatively remove
            the attribute from both entities and replace it with two
            relationships to a third (presumably new) entity with that
            attribute.

Example
To continue with the above example, the attribute *name*, which belongs to the
entity PLAYER, is clearly the same as the attribute *name of goalscorer*, which
belongs to the entity GOAL. Instead of the latter attribute, we can represent the
information as to which player scored which goal by adding a relationship
between the entity GOAL and the entity PLAYER.

Clubs, trophies and individual players may all have commerical sponsorship.
If the three entities CLUB, COMPETITION and PLAYER all have the attribute *name of
sponsor* , this can be simplified by adding a new entity SPONSOR to the model and
replacing the attribute *name of sponsor* in the three entities with three
relationships connecting each in turn with the new entity.

CHECK   The value of one attribute can be deduced from the values of
            one or more other attributes, either of the same entity
            occurrence or of a related entity occurrence.

ACTION   There are two cases. If the value can be directly deduced
            without additional data, such as a total or average, then the
            dependent attribute is redundant and can be removed. If
            additional data are required for the deduction, these data
            would have to be included in the model before the dependent
            attribute could be removed.

Example
To deduce *sign of zodiac* from *date of birth* requires some sort of astrological
table to be included in the model; to deduce *age* from *date of birth* requires the
inclusion of the current date.

Normalization and data redundancy

Some of the checks described in the previous section bear resemblance
to the steps in a bottom–up technique of data modelling, known as
normalization, which produces a so-called *third normal form* (TNF)
data model from an unstructured collection of attributes. For a discussion of normalization, see Appendix I.

The aim of normalization is to remove all redundancy from the data model; the third normal form is completely free of derived or derivable attributes. Is this a useful or practical aim for a data analyst, or is it merely a theoretical exercise?

If a data model is littered or cluttered with duplication and redundancy, it makes it very difficult to understand. However, the attributes that are of interest to the user, particularly at higher management levels, are mostly derived. The model should not ignore these attributes. A data model that includes only basic, indivisable atoms of raw data is like a model of a building that does not include the upper storeys.

The reduction of redundancy should be carried out in moderation, in the same frame of mind as pruning a bush. Deadwood and brambles are to be cut away, but the bush should live on. All repeating groups should be restructured, but duplicated or redundant data should be considered on their merits. A derived attribute should be retained if it is meaningful, or if its removal entails the introduction of some other junk. Record how the attribute can be derived, and keep everyone happy except the theoreticians.

The primary goal of data modelling is to produce a true picture of the system which is clear and easy to understand. The inclusion or exclusion of redundant data should be decided upon this basis and not according to any notion of efficiency. (Let the database designer worry about that.)

Identification of entity occurrences

An entity occurrence must be distinguishable from the other occurrences of the same type. This must be brought out in the data model by specifying a set of relationships and attributes which uniquely identify an entity. A club may be identified by name; if two players happen to have the same name we can still distinguish them by club membership (assuming no club will take on two players with exactly the same name). In other words, the entity CLUB is identified by the attribute *club name,* the entity PLAYER is identified by the attribute *player name* and the relationship between PLAYER and CLUB.

Pieces of paper in offices are usually identified by numbers. An invoice has an invoice number, a delivery has an advice note number, etc. In order to construct a rational numbering scheme (either for a computer system or clerical), it is important to consider the following questions.

Can several deliveries be made to the same customer address on the same day?

Can one invoice cover several deliveries? Can a single delivery be charged on more than one invoice?

Can a delivery cover several orders? Are there blanket orders ('send *x* units per month') or split-delivery orders?

I can recommend no better way to alienate the sympathies of the users than to present them with a numbering scheme which greatly multiplies the amount of paperwork and cancels any benefit of the new system. If the systems designer decrees that the sales order, the advice note, the delivery note and the invoice shall all have the same number (prefixed with the letter 'S', 'A', 'D' and 'V', respectively; it has somehow occurred to him to avoid 'O' and 'I'), the company can only deliver and charge for full orders. If only some of the goods ordered are available, either these must be held until the order can be delivered complete (great for customer relations and internal cashflow!) or the sales order must be amended down to the goods available and a second order issued for the balance.

A systematic data analysis prompts the analyst to ask the right questions; if the designer is told whether each relationship is one-to-one, many-to-one or many-to-many, he will not make the mistake of assuming incorrectly that a relationship is one-to-one.

Often the following situation arises. An entity is usually uniquely identified by a single attribute. However, for a few values of the attribute there are several occurrences of the entity, and a second attribute must be called upon to distinguish between them.

A good example of this may be found in an old fashioned school. A schoolboy is usually uniquely identified by his surname. If there is only one boy in the school with the surname Taylor, he can be referred to unambiguously by the name Taylor.

When his younger brother joins the school, the name Taylor now refers to two different schoolboys. This is resolved by giving each boy a surname-suffix. The elder brother becomes known as Taylor major, the younger is introduced as Taylor minor.

Three points can be noted. First, within his own form, the name Taylor is still used. The suffix is only necessary when the context would allow any boy in the whole school to be referred to. Second, when yet another Taylor joins the school or the eldest Taylor leaves, the suffixes may be changed. Taylor minor may become the new Taylor major. Third, a boy with no brothers is not given a suffix. Whereas a computer system would probably insist that every schoolboy have a suffix, for the sake of uniformity, most teachers are more flexibly minded. The computer would not see anything laughable in the name 'Butcher solus', but a human society would reject this solution as absurd.

Chapter 4

Reconciling Different User Views

Introduction

In this chapter, we shall examine the problems that arise from the fact that the data requirements of an organization vary from one part of the organization to another. Data are generally shared between users whose overall requirements are different.

It is not claimed that all differences can be resolved by the simple logical techniques outlined in this chapter. The data analysts can expect to uncover outright inconsistencies between the assumptions made by the different user departments. Major differences can only be settled by negotiation with and between the users. (This will be discussed in later chapters.) However, minor differences should not cause political problems, and can be catered for by producing a separate user view data model (UVDM) for each user or group of users. The UVDM must be derivable from a unified or global view data model (GVDM). This derivation can be a simple extract, or can involve more complex transformations and calculations.

Differences or incompatibilities of terminology will also be considered, under the heading of synonyms and homonyms.

Who are the users?

Who uses data within an organization?

Let us start by considering a typical manufacturing company. The company is split into functional divisions, each headed by a director. These are as follows:

Production

Sales & Marketing

Finance & Accounts

Personnel

Research & Development

An integrated management information system would be expected to present data in different ways to these five directors (and their staff) because they are interested in different aspects of the company's operations.

Each division may also be further subdivided, which might be apparent from the organizational hierarchy.

However, there are data users that do not appear in this functional hierarchy at all. The management services department will have important data requirements of its own, which will probably be completely unrelated to those of the division it occupies in the hierarchy. (The management services manager often reports to the director of the division that happens to have been computerized first.)

Outside consultants may have requirements for data similar to the management services department, but they may not be allowed to access sensitive information. (Sometimes the reverse is true. Because outside consultants are seen as independent and impartial, they may be privy to things being kept secret for reasons of internal company politics.)

In addition, there may be statutory obligations to provide data to certain outside bodies. Besides the annual audit of the company finances by an independent firm of accountants, the company may be required to provide data to various government departments or other official bodies. It may voluntarily provide data for academic research. This may be in the form of a regular statistical report, or may involve occasional visits from an inspector or researcher.

If the data analyst is not able to interview all these users, he must be able to put himself in their shoes and imagine what their data requirements are likely to be. It may be difficult, for example, to obtain authorization to pay a consultancy fee to the auditors, even though a misconception by the system designers of the auditors' requirements may greatly increase the cost of all subsequent audits. It will be impossible to interview one of the key users: the future systems analyst, who will need statistics on the operation of the new system in order to replace it with a yet newer system.

User views and global views

Each user has his own view of the data he uses. By this we mean that he is interested in certain types of data and not in others, and that he has a certain understanding of how the data he is interested in are structured.

For data to be shared between users, it must be possible to translate between one user view and another. Data may be provided by one user in one form and accessed by other users in different forms.

Furthermore, if the shared data are being stored on a computer database, it must be possible to translate between each user view and the physical configuration of data on magnetic storage media (or computer view).

In order to simplify these translations, we may introduce a central unifying view of the data known as the *global view*. We may depict the relationship between the different views of the data with the diagram in Fig. 4.1, which is loosely based on the recommendations of the ANSI-SPARC database committee. (See the reference to Deen for further discussion.)

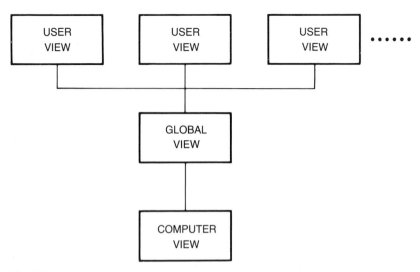

Fig. 4.1

To translate data from one user view to another, or from one user view to the computer view, or from the computer view to a user view, it is necessary to go via the global view.

The advantage of this approach is that it greatly reduces the number of translations or transformations that have to be defined. For n users, the required number of translation definitions is $n + 1$ (assuming that each definition caters for translation in both directions); without the global view it would be necessary to define $n(n + 1)/2$ translations.

Because the global view is the complete and unifying view of the data, the translations are defined in terms of the derivation of each user view from the global view.

The procedure for the data analyst is therefore as follows:

1   talk to users, conduct fact-finding;
2   build a data model of each user view (UVDM), in the form of an entity-relationship diagram with supporting documentation;
3   build a data model from which each UVDM can be derived — this is the global view data model (GVDM);
4   revise each UVDM where necessary and make the derivation from the GVDM explicit.

The production of the computer view, which may include both logical and physical database schemata, is a design activity and will not be discussed here.

Synonyms and homonyms

Working in a particular industry for the first time, the analyst is expected to learn the jargon. Each organization develops subtle variations in the use of language. The workers in one department describe things differently from those of another. The manufacturing stage that is 'output' for the bodyshop may be 'input' for the paintshop.

When two words turn out to have the same meaning, this should be recognized by the analyst and documented as *synonymy*. When the same word is used with different meanings, these must be differentiated clearly by the analyst and documented as *homonymy*.

The commonest example of homonymy is the word 'order'. In a large manufacturing company, there may be purchase orders, work orders, parts orders, sales orders, maintenance orders, and so on. Usually people just say 'order' for any of these; the context makes it plain which kind of order they mean. When a salesman talks of orders, he means sales orders; when he has to talk of purchase orders he will use the full name. For a buyer the reverse would be true.

The data analyst must rise above the confusion. Even if he decides that all these kinds of order are structurally similar and constructs a model with entity type ORDER, of which SALES ORDER, PARTS ORDER, etc. would be *entity subtypes,* he must take care to distinguish these subtypes according to their different functions and uses.

When two terms in common use are identified to be synonyms by the data analyst, it is not necessary for the two terms to be exactly equivalent. They may refer to overlapping or adjacent sets of things. What matters is that the two terms are *essentially* equivalent, in other words that they can be combined for the purposes of data modelling.

How, then, does the analyst decide that two terms are synonyms and should be modelled as a single entity, rather than as two entities? He will observe that both are identified in a similar way, that both are related to other entities in similar ways, and that both have more or less the same list of attributes.

How does the analyst decide that one term is homonymic and refers to two distinct entities? He will observe that the occurrences divide into two or more types. These types will have different lists of attributes and different relationships to other entities. They will probably be processed by wholly different functions.

The analyst is often faced with a situation where all of the users' terminology is ambiguous or unsuitable. He is forced to construct or invent names for the entities in his data model. This must be done with great tact and sensibility. The names he invents should be easily understood by the user, should in fact be based on the users' own vocabulary, but should not be confused with any previously used ambiguous terms.

The best way to clarify an ambiguous term is with a prefix, e.g. 'purchase order' instead of 'order'. More difficult is the case when the analyst needs a name that is less specific, more generally applicable than the terms commonly used. For example, an accomodation agency may deal with both flats and houses. If the analyst decides that only one entity is required to model flats and houses together, he may need to find a new name for this entity such as 'dwelling'. If offices and shops are also to be included in the model, a yet more general name must be found.

If the scope of the data analysis includes an existing computer system, the terms to be analysed may include abbreviated codes. PORDNO may turn out to be a synonym of PURNUM, both being code names for purchase order number.

Terms for relationships and attributes may be subject to synonymy and homonymy; this is dealt with in similar fashion.

Simple conflicts resolved

The simplest form of derivation is based on inclusion or exclusion. Each UVDM is a straight extract from the GVDM. Anything that appears in the UVDM must be modelled by the same construct as in the GVDM.

To restrict oneself to this form of derivation makes the derivation itself trivial. As long as the terminology is consistent, there is no need to document the derivation explicitly. Furthermore, several computer software packages, such as commerically available data dictionaries, are only able to handle this form of derivation.

However, it is a very severe limitation, as we shall see when we consider other forms of derivation. The GVDM is much more difficult to produce and maintain.

In most cases it is obvious which entities, attributes and relationships are of interest to a particular user. Often, however, the requirements of users are overlapping but apparently inconsistent. Particular problems arise as a result of the time dimension. Different users are interested in entities at different stages of the entity life cycle. An example of such an information conflict follows.

In one company, the paperwork associated with a sales order typically took several weeks. This included the time to validate the terms of the order officially and to sign-off the contract. This was of no consequence to the sales and marketing departments; they would want to have the order included in their reported results for the month in which the sales effort for this order was completed and the customer placed the order. Of course, in a few cases the contractual negotiations between the customer and the legal department would break down, or the terms of the order would be substantially changed, but usually these negotiations were a formality and were ignored. The production department were not allowed to start work on the job until the contract had been finally signed-off. They would therefore want the order included in the New Order Report for the month in which the contract was signed. Each department wants the order included in its performance and planning reports at a different time.

If this problem is recognized during the data analysis it can be easily resolved, for example by recognizing as different attributes the total *orders placed but not yet signed-off* and the total *orders placed and signed-off*. These attributes may both be derived from the attribute of ORDER that indicates the order's signed-off status.

Structural conflicts resolved

Besides the simple suppression of entities, attributes and relationships from the GVDM to produce a UVDM, it may be appropriate to change some constructs, so that some of the entities, relationships and attributes of the UVDM do not appear as such in the GVDM, but are derivable from the GVDM.

We have already mentioned derived attributes. If a single user is interested in individual production figures and in the total production figures, the latter are derivable from the former and need not be included in his UVDM. Suppose, however, that a particular user is interested in summary data, such as totals and averages, without being interested in the individual figures from which the summary data are derived. It is then appropriate to include in his user view only the data he is interested in.

The derivable data are excluded from the GVDM as being redundant, but they must be available to the user and are therefore included in his UVDM. The derivation of the UVDM from the GVDM must therefore specify how each derived attribute is calculated.

Similar considerations apply to derived relationships. Let us consider a couple of examples. Suppose the GVDM contains the portion given in Fig. 4.2.

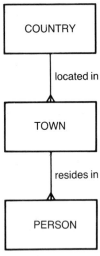

Fig. 4.2

One user may not be interested in towns at all, but needs to know which people reside in which countries. His UVDM contains the portion given in Fig. 4.3.

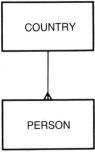

Fig. 4.3

The relationship between country and person is derived from two relationships and one entity in the GVDM. It is not included in the GVDM because it would be redundant there. It is however included in the UVDM.

The following example shows a relationship being derived from an attribute and a relationship.

One user is interested in all the marriages contracted by a person in his/her life. His UVDM therefore contains the portion given in Fig. 4.4.

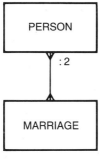

Fig. 4.4

(The :2 indicates that at most two persons are implicated in an ongoing marriage.)

Another user is interested only in current marriages. His UVDM therefore contains the simpler portion given in Fig. 4.5.

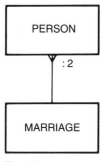

Fig. 4.5

The first is more comprehensive than the second. The second can be derived from the first by ignoring all marriages that have been annulled (which is an attribute of marriage, perhaps linked to date of divorce or widowhood). Therefore the first, more general model is incorporated into the GVDM. For the UVDMs that require the second, more simple model, the derivation is straightforward.

Exercise 6

Under what circumstances might the four models in Fig. 4.6 be valid? If four users had different data requirements corresponding to the four different models, how could this be reconciled?

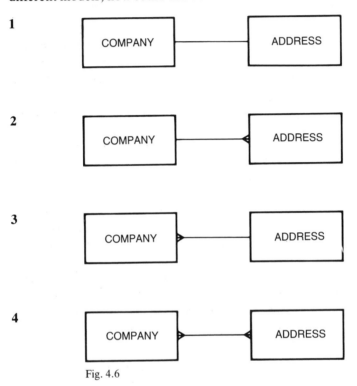

Fig. 4.6

Chapter 5

Documenting the Data Model

Introduction

The most stimulating part of the data analysis exercise is what might be called the whiteboard fight. A small group of analysts (perhaps including one or two co-opted users) take it in turns to draw boxes and lines on a whiteboard or blackboard, pushing and pulling the data model until the structure is satisfactory.

However, a data model consisting only of an E-R diagram is not of much use. A box may be labelled, but each person may interpret the label differently. Full definitions and other documentation are essential to complete the data model. This chapter describes the more important aspects of the data structure that should be recorded.

The motivation for discovering and recording these aspects of data structure is sometimes explicitly related to the needs of the database designer and implementer. Obviously, if the data model is being produced for some other purpose, it may be unnecessary to spend a lot of time on such details.

Documenting the data model on paper is an unnecessary chore, when a suitable data dictionary is available. An automated data dictionary will allow all of these *data about data* (sometimes called *metadata*) to be stored, maintained and enquired upon.

Need for precise definition of all terms in model

Many badly designed computer systems give incorrect results because the meaning of certain data items was not consistently understood across the whole system. Data analysis demands that every entity, relationship and attribute be precisely defined. Consider the following questions, which refer to our sports example. It is clear that the designer of the various subsystems and the users of the whole system, must agree on the answer. If left as undocumented assumptions, the chances are that misunderstandings arise.

Does a junior, taken on trial for 6 months, count as a player?
Does a friendly game count as a match?

If a player acts as substitute or twelfth man, does he count as having 'played in' the match?

Is a player's nationality based on his international allegiance, his country of birth or his passport?

One way of defining a part of the data model is to describe as precisely as possible the information that is being represented. We can avail ourselves of the Wittgenstinian doctrine *meaning is use,* which we can interpret in this context as saying that the information is to be described in terms of the use of the information.

As an illustration of the need for defining entities, let us consider a data model for a restaurant. The data system includes the passing of the order from the guests by the waiter to the chef and the activities associated with settling the bill.

What is a meal? There are several possible definitions.

1   Any combination of dishes from the menu that could be eaten in partial sequence on one occasion by one person, e.g.

> Avocado Mousse
> Turbot Poche with New Potatoes and Salad
> Cheese & Biscuits
> Coffee

This meal comprises six dishes. They are not in strict sequence because the main course arrives together with vegetables. They are in partial sequence because the main course follows the hors-d'oeuvre and precedes the dessert (if taken).

2   A meal is what is eaten by one person at one sitting.

If two people order Avocado, Turbot, etc., are we to count this as *one* occurrence of meal connected with *two* occurrences of some other entity, or as *two* occurrences of meal? This depends on whether we have chosen definition **1** or **2**.

3   A meal is a collection of dishes assembled onto one bill.

When the accountant sends all the slips off to the credit card company, he will regard each as representing one meal.

4   A meal is what is eaten by one paying guest at one sitting,

i.e. the same as **2** but ignoring food consumed by restaurant staff.

5   A meal is what is eaten at one table at one sitting.

The waiter taken an order from one table: three hors-d'oeuvres, four main courses, various vegetables, and so on. The chef must strive to deliver the appropriate dishes at the same time.

6   A meal is a mode of eating, determined by the time of the day, e.g.

> breakfast
> luncheon

dinner

supper

This definition may be useful in working out the shift patterns of the waiters. Although this entity might in practice be loosely called 'meal' it would be more appropriately called something else.

Many more definitions of 'meal' could be conceived. Moreover, it is possible that all these definitions be in use in one restaurant.

If we sit in the corner of the restaurant for a week, counting the meals and recording other statistics, we will come up with a different total according to which definition we use. We must also decide what to do in exceptional cases: when the guest orders but does not stay to eat; when he eats but does not stay to pay; when he changes tables.

Because data analysis forces us to ask 'Can a meal have several bills?', etc., it forces us to confront and resolve the confusion. The definition should always aim to determine how many entity occurrences are present in a given situation.

Exercise 7

Consider the following definition of the entity FREIGHT SHIPMENT: 'a movement of goods from a source location to a destination on behalf of a customer'. What problems are likely to arise from this definition in practice?

Data accuracy

Suppose that the system uses an attribute of the environment (an external variable) which is not accurately or reliably known within the system.

For example, the sales director may want to know the company's *market share* of a particular product. There may be several techniques of estimating the sales figures of the company's competitors: market surveys, either published in the trade press or privately commissioned, reports from salesmen (analysis of lost sales), industrial espionage, company reports, etc. The market analyst will come up with an informed guess on the basis of as many of these sources as are available to him.

How do we model this process? (See Fig. 5.1.) The analyst compares a number of competing information items and generates a new INFO ITEM (by weighted average?) with a higher reliability than any of the input items.

If there are several analysts doing this (their results to be consolidated

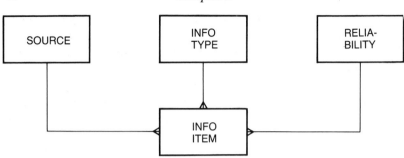

Fig. 5.1

as a second-level weighted average, say), we need an involuted re-lationship on the INFO ITEM so that the analysis results can be separately recorded and checked (see Fig. 5.2).

If the information item is raw data, its reliability depends on the source and type. Feedback will allow the reliability rating of each source with respect to each type to be checked. If the item is produced by an analyst from several other items, the reliability will depend on the reliability of the items the new item is based on, the skill of the analyst and/or the weighting he/she is using, and perhaps other factors. It is unlikely that this process will be easily automated, that human judge-ment will be altogether eliminated.

Another reason for data inaccuracy may be the urgency of the requirement for information. In one direct marketing organization, the number of replies received each day to a mailshot promotion was charted on a graph. After only a few days it was possible to make a rough estimate of the total number of replies that would be received.

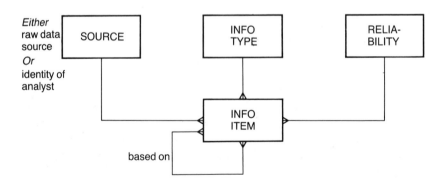

Fig. 5.2

This estimate was used to evaluate the promotion and to start designing the next promotion. It was not possible to wait until all the replies had been received before making any decisions, as this might delay the next promotion by several weeks.

In such situations, a trade-off is made between the accuracy of the information and its timeliness. Management must decide whether it needs to wait for the final set of figures or can make do with a provisional set.

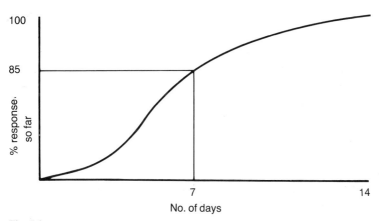

Fig. 5.3

Assuming that the pattern of response to a marketing campaign follows the curve shown in Fig. 5.3, an estimate of the total response can be made after 7 days by multiplying the response so far by 100/85.

In fact, the graph cannot be drawn as accurately as this. The percentage that will be received after 7 days will be between 80% and 90%. Therefore the estimate of total response will be a rough figure between 100/90 and 100/80 of the response so far.

Data ownership

The model of a shared data system must clearly show the extent of this sharing. Obviously, not every data item is to be made public, even within the organization. The classic example of this is payroll information. Only the payroll clerks are allowed to know how much an employee is paid, and only an employee's manager is allowed to increase his wages. Against each restricted-access data item, therefore, must be documented:

1 who is allowed to read the data item (in terms of role within the organization, rather than by name — if possible, document the organization *functions* for which the data item is required);
2 who is allowed to create/update/delete the data item (also in terms of organizational role — again, try to specify the functions that involve a change to this data item).

Such privacy considerations may apply to attributes or to entities, or for that matter to relationships.

Other ownership considerations, which should be documented for each data item where appropriate, are as follows.

Source   Where do the data get generated or become known? (Some data result from decisions; in that case the person responsible for the decision should be specified.)

Availability When and how do the data get generated or become known?

Retention   How long do the data need to be kept for? What procedures are used to archive or scrap data that are no longer required?

Data usage

The documentation of the data model must make clear what the *relevance* is of each part of the model. Most data items will be required by one or more specific functions within the system; nothing should be included in the final model without an explicit rationale.

A data item may be processed by the system in various ways. It may be

1 examined logically or compared with other data items (this may include validity testing or key sorting);
2 used in an arithmetical calculation (this may include statistical or algebraic equations);
3 passed through the sytem without change.

Typically, data will have a number of *destinations*. Besides the intermediate processes or functions that use the data, there may be several potential end-users, which can include both humans and computers.

Data volumes

In order to design an efficient data processing system, it is essential to have some idea of the quantities of data involved and the frequency of access.

We therefore need to estimate the number of occurrences of each entity, relationship and attribute, the number of new occurrences per time period and the frequency of each type of access (read, create, update, delete) for each data item. For the last set of estimates, we need to identify the business functions for which an access to the data item is required and multiply the frequency that each such business function is carried out by the (average) number of accesses to the given data item involved in each execution of the business function.

Static or slow-moving entities may be sized by estimating the actual number of occurrences, together with any anticipated growth rate (e.g. 2000 customers, plus 100 new customers per annum).

Dynamic or transaction entities may be sized by estimating the rate of creation of occurrences together with the life-span of each occurrence (e.g. 500 orders placed per week, orders take an average of 2 months from placement to completion).

It may be necessary to record maximum and minimum as well as average volumes. The analyst should be aware of seasonal fluctuations of transaction rates, and should discover what peaks of data creation rates may occur.

If there is not enough time for the data analyst to produce estimates of all data volumes, he must identify the critical data items and at least produce estimates of these.

Documentation of relationships

The most important fact that must be recorded for each relationship is the simplest one: what the relationship actually consists of. What does it mean to say that an occurrence of one entity is related in this way to one or more occurrences of another entity? The relationship description, just as the description of the other parts of the data model, must include a precise definition. Furthermore, the information represented by the relationship must have a source (where does the information come from?), a destination (where/how is the information used?) and a relevance (why is it needed?).

Also to be recorded is the permanence of each relationship. Over its lifetime, can an entity occurrence change the other entity occurrences it is related to? If so, how often and under what circumstances? With marriage, for example, it would be worth knowing the actual frequency of divorce and remarriage, as well as the legal conditions and religious constraints.

Additional facts to be recorded for each relationship are the *degree* (whether the relationship is one-to-one, one-to-many or many-to-many) and the *optionality* (whether every occurrence of the first entity type must be related to one or more occurrences of the second entity type and vice versa). These facts can be recorded in a simple table (Fig. 5.4).

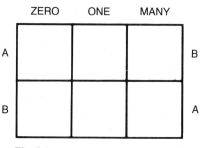

Fig. 5.4

This table is to be read as follows. Ticks in the first line of the table indicate whether an occurrence of the entity type A is allowed to be related to zero, one or many occurrences of the entity type B. If there is a tick in the ZERO column of the first line, it means that an occurrence of A does not have to be related to any occurrences of the entity type B; the relationship is then said to be *optional* with respect to A. If there is no such tick, then each occurrence of A must be related to at least one occurrence of B, in which case the relationship is said to be *mandatory* with respect to A. Ticks in the second line indicate whether an occurrence of B is allowed to be related to zero, one or many occurrences of A.

Instead of completing the table with ticks, showing mere possibilities, the table can be completed with percentages, showing the relative frequencies of the different possibilities. In addition, the average or maximum numbers of occurrences of B related to a single occurrence of A, and vice versa, can be recorded.

Documentation of attributes

The attributes of each entity type must be listed and defined. Special attention is devoted to those attributes that are used to identify entities (known as *key* attributes). Some attributes may not have a meaningful value for every occurrence of the entity type, and the conditions for this will be noted.

An attribute has a range of *possible* values. This range may depend on the values of other attributes or on the existence of certain entity or relationship occurrences. Some values may be more likely than others (e.g. 99% of employees are aged between 21 and 60). So we also have a range of *probable* values.

In designing a system, validation rules are included to help prevent incorrect data from entering the system. These rules are of two kinds. A user will be prevented from entering data outside the range of possible values (error validation); he may be cautioned against, but not prevented from, entering data outside the range of probable values (warning validation). The systems designer may, for example, require that improbable input be specially confirmed as correct. These validation rules are based on the documentation of the attribute.

Attention must also be paid to the degree of fineness or precision of the data, sometimes referred to as the *grain* of the data. In other words, the most specific value of each attribute should be stated, together with any relevant groups or classifications of values.

Logical data dependency

The existence of one data item may depend on the existence or value of other data items. For example, a person can only have a driving licence (number) if he or she is over 16. Such logical dependencies can be indefinitely complicated. Attempts have been made to develop diagrammatic conventions to show logical dependencies between relationships, e.g. by means of arcs and dotted lines. Experience shows that such conventions do not work. They are difficult to remember, and can only be applied to the simplest cases. There is usually no substitute for describing the dependency in precise, logical sentences.

Chapter 6

Data Access

Introduction

The E-R diagram and associated documentation, which have been described in previous chapters, give us a model of the logical structure of information within an organization. This chapter describes how the model can be extended to show how the information is used and updated. In addition to the static model, we need a set of dynamic models, known as data access models (DAMs). These show the usage and updating of information by each business function. The analysis of the business functions themselves goes outside the scope of this book. But we shall discuss the ways that a function can access information, and how this can be documented within the context of the logical data model itself.

Need to describe access

Why is it necessary to analyse the access of data as well as the structure? There are two reasons. The first is that the data access models provide a valuable cross-check against the data structure model. If an important business function is unable to access the data as it requires, the data structure model may need to be revised.

The second reason is that the access models provide valuable information to the database designer, who must know the access requirements of a database as well as the structural requirements. The choices made by the database designer may give faster or more efficient response to certain types of user request, while other types of user request may be slower or less efficient. He therefore needs to know which types of request are most frequent, and which areas are most critical to the performance of the whole system.

Postponement of navigation

What the analyst is always concerned to do is to provide a logical model of what has to be done. To specify how it is to be done is inappropriate during the analysis stage of a systems development project; 'how' decisions should be left to the design stage.

According to some methodologies, the data accesses required for each business function should be specified in terms of *navigation*. This is analogous to the navigation of a CODASYL database by a *COBOL* program and consists of a list of instructions that describe an *access path* through the data model. Such a description might be of the following form:

FIND such-and-such occurrences OF ENTITY A
FOLLOW RELATIONSHIP AB TO FIND AN OCCURRENCE OF ENTITY B
etc.

Equivalently, a copy of the E-R diagram is superimposed with arrows to show how the data access should hop from one entity to another.

Clearly, if a *COBOL* program is to be written as an implementation of the particular business function, some decisions must be taken at some stage concerning the order in which records are retrieved and updated. The decisions made at the database design stage may force the database to be accessed according to a particular navigation path, or there may be several possible paths. In the latter case, the optimum path can be chosen according to the priorities of systems design, such as performance. It is contrary to the basic separation between analysis and design for any such decision to be taken prematurely, during the analysis stage.

There is no point in tying the hands of the database designer, who may have legitimate reasons for providing or not providing 'short cuts' for the navigation of the database. If a function is specified in terms that assume the presence or absence of a particular short cut, it may have to be respecified during or after the database design. Alternatively, if the computer system development uses a fourth-generation programming language, the navigation may be decided by the computer software itself. It may be possible for an access path to be selected at run-time, given an appropriate algorithm.

An analysis model must be independent of the systems design. It follows that an access model produced by the data analyst cannot include details of the navigation paths, but should include enough information about the business function to allow the navigation paths to be specified at the right time, either by the systems designer or chosen automatically by the computer.

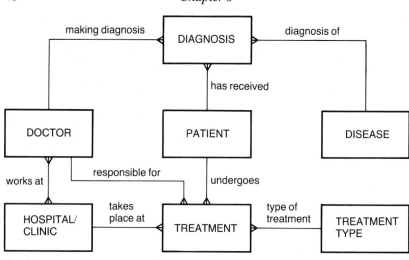

Fig. 6.1

Retrieval access description

For this section, and the following, we shall use the entity-relationship model in Fig. 6.1, which is for a health care system.

A doctor diagnoses a particular disease in a patient. This is represented by the entity DIAGNOSIS. (It is clearly possible for a doctor to diagnose several diseases in the same patient: this involves several occurrences of DIAGNOSIS.) The patient is then treated at a hospital or clinic by a doctor, who need not be the same as the doctor that diagnosed the patient's condition. This is represented by the entity TREATMENT.

We shall assume that the relationship between TREATMENT TYPE and DISEASE is outside the scope of this system. This relationship, indicating the suitability of certain types of treatment for certain diseases or combinations of diseases, is a genuine, albeit complicated, one. It is usually a matter for the expertise of the doctors. A so-called expert system would involve a computerized representation of such information. For the purposes of this example, this shall be ignored.

There are many kinds of questions that can be answered using the information contained in this model.

1   What treatment(s) has patient X had?
2   Which patients has doctor Y diagnosed the condition of?
3   Which hospitals have patients suffering from disease Z?
4   Which doctors work at more than one hospital or clinic?
5   Which doctor has the highest pass-on rate (i.e. diagnosing the

conditions of patients who are subsequently treated by a different doctor)?

6 What diseases do doctors themselves get? (This question demands an analysis of those patients that happen also to be doctors.)

In concerning ourselves with the access of data, which may be to answer such questions as these, we should try not to commit ourselves to a particular way of presenting the answer. One reason is that matters of sequence or format are not relevant at this stage. Another reason is that complex enquiries can be built from such simple questions. Consider the following:

7 What treatment(s) has each patient had, whose condition has been diagnosed by doctor Y?

This enquiry can be analysed into two components, which are the questions **1** and **2** listed above. This book recommends a modular approach to describing data access, in which the data access model (DAM) for question **7** is built using the DAMs for questions **1** and **2**.

For a retrieval data access, only two things must be specified. First, which attributes are to be retrieved? Second, which entity occurrence or occurrences are they to be retrieved from? There are three styles of retrieval data access: *singular,* in which the attributes are retrieved from a single occurrence of an entity type; *plural*, in which the attributes are retrieved from several occurrences of a single entity type; and *complex*, in which the attributes are retrieved from occurrences of several entity types. A complex data access is broken down into simple data accesses, which may be either singular or plural.

One problem that often arises with formally specified query languages is that there are syntactic restrictions on the use of singular and plural. For example, we might want to ask:

8 How many patients are currently being treated at the hospital that doctor Y works at?

Because some doctors work at more than one hospital or clinic, this query may or may not be meaningful, according to the identity of doctor Y. If doctor Y belongs to the majority of doctors, working at only one hospital, then question **8** is perfectly meaningful. If doctor Y works in many hospitals, then more information is needed to identify the particular hospital, before the question can be answered.

Some formal languages disallow such questions as **8** because they are not meaningful in all circumstances. Even such questions as

9 Which doctor diagnosed the largest number of lumbago complaints last month?

are disallowed, because it is possible for two doctors to tie for first place.

It is clear that users want to ask that sort of question, therefore the analysis of data access should allow for it. The data access models are therefore informal, with a deliberately vague syntax. Translation of these data access models into a formal computer-readable language is a job for a programmer, and is beyond the scope of this book.

There are four basic ways of denoting entity occurrences.
1 Given an entity occurrence already denoted, use a relationship to denote another entity occurrence.
E.g. given an occurrence of TREATMENT, we can refer to the DOCTOR responsible for the TREATMENT. Because *responsible for* is a many-to-one relationship, this denotes a unique occurrence of DOCTOR.
2 Given an entity occurrence already denoted, use a relationship to denote a set of entity occurrences.
E.g. given an occurrence of HOSPITAL, we can refer to all the TREATMENTS that take place there.
3 Given a set of entity occurrences already denoted, use a relationship to denote another set of entity occurrences.
E.g. using the set of TREATMENTS that take place in a given HOSPITAL, we can refer to the set of PATIENTS that are undergoing TREATMENT in the HOSPITAL.
4 Given a set of entity occurrences, select one or more occurrences according to the value of an attribute or combination of attributes.
E.g. using the set of all DOCTORS, we can refer to the DOCTOR with surname = Jeckell.
E.g. using the set of all PATIENTS undergoing TREATMENT in a given HOSPITAL, we can refer to those PATIENTS aged over 65 (if male) or aged over 60 (if female).

These four ways of denoting entity occurrences can be combined indefinitely.

Consider the following example:

FIND ALL DOCTORS WHO HAVE CARRIED OUT SURGERY ON LUMBAGO PATIENTS.

This is clearly a complex data access. It involves many entity types, including DISEASE (i.e. lumbago) and TREATMENT TYPE (i.e. surgery).

A top–down analysis will start as follows.

Has lumbago may be regarded as a derived attribute of PATIENT; *has carried out surgery on* may be regarded as a derived relationship between DOCTOR and PATIENT. We want the set of DOCTORS bearing this derived relationship to PATIENTS possessing this derived attribute. All that remains is to define the derived attribute *has lumbago* and the derived relationship *has carried out surgery on*. These definitions will require further data access models to be specified.

The data access model for *has lumbago* depends on the entity type DIAGNOSIS. We have assumed that a patient has lumbago if a diagnosis of lumbago has been made; in other words, *has lumbago* is equivalent to the existence of an appropriate DIAGNOSIS. Therefore we define that an occurrence of PATIENT *has lumbago* if it is related to an occurrence of DIAGNOSIS *of lumbago*. We also define that an occurrence of DIAGNOSIS is *of lumbago* if it is related to the occurrence of DISEASE named lumbago.

We can document this schematically as follows, using variables A, B, ... to refer to sets of entity occurrences.

Doctors A	defined as	all DOCTORS related via *has carried out surgery on* to at least one PATIENT who *has lumbago*.
has lumbago	defined as	attribute of PATIENT such that it is related via *has received* to at least one DIAGNOSIS that is *of lumbago*.
of lumbago	defined as	attribute of DIAGNOSIS such that it is related via *diagnosis of* to the DISEASE named lumbago.
has carried out surgery on		left as an exercise for the reader (Exercise 8).

The set A of doctors defined above may be referred to in a yet more complex data access model, or it may be converted into an output list for displaying or printing.

It is obviously possible on many projects to agree symbols and abbreviations to make this document shorter.

Modification access description

Stored data on a computer system may need updating for two reasons. The first reason is that, as result of an error, the data do not correctly represent the entities in the real world they are supposed to represent. The second reason is that, as a result of a change in the real world, the data no longer correctly represent the real world.

Although the designer of a computer system must be aware of all the mistakes the computer user may make, which may cause him to require adjustment to the computer files, the systems analyst is primarily concerned with the representation of genuine changes in the real world.

This section therefore concentrates on the second of the two reasons for update and ignores error correction.

What kinds of change in the real world may require modification to the data? Let us consider a few typical events.

(i)   A new patient joins the system.

(ii) A diagnosis is made.

(iii) A treatment is started.

(iv) A doctor hands responsibility for a patient to another doctor.

(v)   A patient moves to another hospital.

(vi) A doctor moves to another hospital.

Just as with retrieval access, modification access can be complex and be capable of being broken down into simpler components. When a doctor changes hospital, for example, many of his patients must either change hospital or change doctor.

There are three basic updates that can be made to the data.

1   Establish a new occurrence of an entity, with values for its attributes and with relationships between it and certain denoted entity occurrences.

2   Change the attributes of a denoted entity occurrence.

3   Change the relationship between a denoted entity occurrence and other entity occurrences.

Although deletion is an important operation on a computer database, it does not represent anything in the real world. When an object ceases to exist, or a person dies, the information about that object or person continues to exist. Information is, in principle, immortal. The most that can be done is to identify events that diminish the importance or relevance of information; data are archived or scrapped not when they become meaningless (never), but when they become not worth keeping (sooner or later).

Each update function [for example (i) – (vi) above] should be documented in terms of the data accesses required. The three basic update operations may be used, as well as the denotation of entity occurrences, which uses the retrieval access techniques described in the previous section.

Chapter 7

Uses for Data Analysis

Introduction

The reasons for doing data analysis have so far not been made explicit. The purpose of this chapter is to outline some of the ways in which a data model can be useful. Data models can be used or referred to at all stages of the systems development cycle, from feasibility study through to implementation. System prototypes should be based on properly analysed data requirements. If information is to be regarded as an accountable asset, a data model is required in order to evaluate this asset.

The strategy study

Plans for the management services area of an organization are usually drawn up several years in advance. A complex new computer system can take up to 5 years from conception to final implementation. An information strategy must be worked out for the long-term provision of management information. A complex collection of user requirements may be satisfied by several separate or interconnecting systems, each of which would be developed as a separate project. These projects could be scheduled in parallel, with teams working side-by-side, or in series, with one team working on one project after another. Most DP departments develop systems in a more complicated way; this requires strategic planning by DP management.

A global data model for the whole organization can be used to divide the whole system into subsystems. A subsystem should be as self-contained as possible; the objective is to minimize the interconnections between the subsystems (and thus to simplify the interfaces). An analysis of the data model can be carried out to divide the model into relatively self-contained 'clusters'. Usually this is done by hand. However, computer software is available to divide any network structure into clusters, and this can be applied to very large data models. The software relies on mathematical techniques of cluster analysis. Formal application of cluster analysis is only required when the system is too complex to be divided by common-sense methods. When the system has been properly divided into subsystems, the global data model can be used to make recommendations as to future system development. In particular, decisions as to which subsystems to computerize, and in what sequence, should be made partly on the basis of the required communications between the subsystems.

Application system evaluation

Every data processing system assumes a particular data structure. Even if a system has not been designed on the basis of a proper data analysis, the system itself can be analysed in order to discover the *implicit* data model. We can produce an implicit data model for a working or proposed system simply by documenting and structuring the data assumptions in a standard format. By doing this, we can easily spot any incoherence in these assumptions, which may have been overlooked when the assumptions were left undocumented or unchecked. By criticizing the implicit data model, we can point out potential improvements in the system.

In the selection of an application package, for example, the available packages can be compared by comparing their implicit data models with the model that represents the data requirements. There is no point in buying the fastest system, or the cheapest, if the user's data requirements are not met; the best way of judging the extent to which the requirements are met is to strip off the features that depend on the particular hardware or software and look at the logical structure, i.e. at the implicit data model. It is rare to find a package that fits the requirements exactly; the comparison can be used to estimate the costs that would be incurred in installing a package that does not quite fit, which may include software tailoring or additional clerical effort.

(A good package supplier will of course save you the trouble of working out the implicit data model; if the package has been developed properly, the model will already be available.)

Selection of data management software

Another use of the data model is to evaluate the systems software. If the currently used file management system would not be adequate to support an implementation of the data model, it may be necessary to consider the development or purchase of a database management system. The data management software must fit the logical data requirements, although this is clearly not the only criterion for selection. Nor is it an absolute criterion; an ingenious designer can usually find a way to implement any data requirements using any software system, but it is better if such ingenuity is not needed.

Systems design

The most common reason for carrying out systems analysis is as a prelude to designing a new system. The data model is invaluable to any database designer, but should also be used when one is designing conventional files. The design decisions should be taken with the aim of optimizing systems performance, given the unambiguous requirements and assumptions clearly laid out in the data model.

If the data model includes items of marginal relevance to the organization, it will be necessary to compare the expected benefit of having access to the information with the additional cost of collecting and maintaining it.

Further discussion of the design and implementation of a data system based on a properly documented data model can be found in the next chapter.

Data set-up

The implementation of a computer system usually involves the setting-up of data before the system can operate.

This 'starting set' of data can include master file data, look-up tables of various kinds and all forms of static data. Depending on the implementation strategy, it may also include data about 'transactions-in-progress'.

The starting set may be assembled from several sources, including conversion of files from an existing computer system, existing documents to be entered into the computer, and new data to be created by decision or research.

Various problems can arise at this stage, which a proper data analysis will have identified:

1 data items from different sources do not correspond one-to-one (which may lead to data records being incomplete);

2 code numbers on corresponding entity occurrences do not match;

3 data are inconsistent between two or more sources;

4 supposedly unique entities are duplicated in different sources (e.g. in merging the customer lists for each sales area, we find some customers appearing more than once).

With a large system, or with large amounts of data to be set up, a staged implementation may be appropriate. The data analyst should be in a position to advise an appropriate segmentation of the data, for example by geographical area of business, or product group.

Chapter 8

Implementation of the Data Model

Introduction

It may be thought that the data model, consisting of entities, relationships and attributes, can be implemented as a database without further ado. What is an entity, after all, but a fancy name for a record? What is an attribute other than a fancy name for a field? The data model looks exactly the same as the logical database design.

This is a misconception. The database designer earns his salary. A relationship can be implemented as a set, relation, network, link or chain, by including the key of one record as a field in another, or with a separate look-up table. The choice depends on considerations of volumes of data, required performance and, above all, how often the represented information is used by the system.

Ideally, the choice of the database management software should be postponed until the data analysis is complete (a rare luxury). The data model must be independent of the proposed implementation, it must allow anything from sequential files to CODASYL, from DL/1 to SQL, from filing cabinets overflowing paper to bubbles.

Database principles

The Conference on Data Systems Languages, known as CODASYL, has established the following principles for database management systems.

1   Data definitions should be removed from application programs.
2   Data definitions should be centralized in one location.
3   Relationships between records can be defined.
4   The physical characteristics of these records and relationships should be separated from the data definitions.
5   Tailored user views of the database should be made available to users.
6   Administration of the database should be centralized.
7   The integrity of the database should be maintained in the event of user errors and hardware or software failures.
8   Multiple users should have concurrent access to the data.

These principles apply to all databases, not only to those that are structured according to the CODASYL recommendations.

Types of database

Suppose that we want to store information about people, together with information about the town they live in.

The simplest file structure for this is the *flat file*. For each person, a record is stored. Each record is of the same format and contains person data and town data (Fig. 8.1).

Fig. 8.1

The trouble with this structure is that some data are being stored many times over. The town data are repeated in each record for persons living in the town. This data redundancy has the following disadvantages:

1 storage space is being wasted by storing the same data more than once;

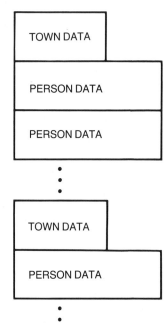

Fig. 8.2

2 when the town information needs to be changed, a simple update operation must be carried out not once but for each record containing the data;

3 if for any reason the town data should differ from one copy to the next, it is impossible to decide which is the correct version.

To remove the data redundancy, one strategy is to sort the file so that all records containing data for the same town are together. The town data are then stored only once (Fig. 8.2).

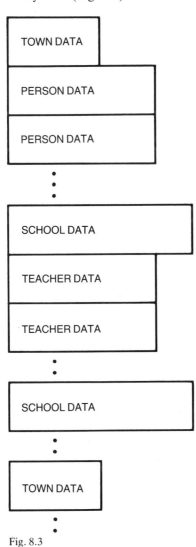

Fig. 8.3

This is a *hierarchical* structure. We now have two record types; the relationship between town records and person records is determined by the sequence of the file.

It is clearly possible to extend this hierarchical structure to include further record types, as in Fig. 8.3. Following each town record there are a number of person records followed by a number of school records. Each school record may be followed by a number of teacher records. This is represented as a hierarchical schema, as in Fig. 8.4.

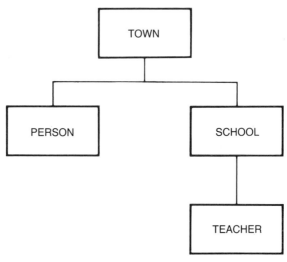

Fig. 8.4

It should be obvious that it would be impossible to store this information using a simple single-format flat file such as we opened this section with. A hierarchical database management system such as IMS can be regarded as a sophistication of this structure.

Another way of storing the information is as a set of tables. Each entity type may be represented by a table of data, with the lines of the table representing the entity occurrences and the columns of the table representing the different attributes.

The school table, for example, could be as shown in Fig. 8.5. In addition to the attribute columns, extra columns are included (School Code, Town Code) to enable the relationships between entities to be represented. Each entry on the teacher table will contain a School Code, showing which school each teacher teaches at.

This is how a *relational database* is structured.

SCHOOL CODE	SCHOOL NAME	TOWN CODE	NUMBER OF PUPILS
M37	MANCHESTER	BIR	714
S14	ST. RHODES	LON	417
M03	MERTON GRAMMAR	LON	174
G71	GRANTHAM HIGH	GRA	471

Fig. 8.5

A *network database* is a compromise between the hierarchical and the relational. The relationships between records are represented not by the position of the record, nor by explicit codes used as cross-references, but by internally maintained pointers.

A one-to-many relationship between two entity types is represented by a chain of pointers between records, known as a *set*. A record of one record type, known as the *owner*, is linked to several records of another record type, known as *members*. A network database schema is drawn in the same way as a data model, except for the convention that a set is drawn as an arrow from one record to another (Fig. 8.6).

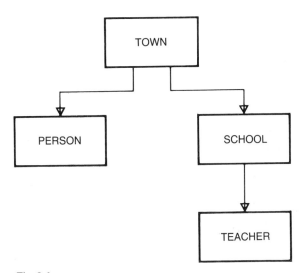

Fig. 8.6

So far this appears to be similar to the hierarchical schema. However, there is no restriction to the sets that can be included in a network database, provided that each set links two record types in a one-to-many fashion.

So we can simplify this schema by observing that a teacher is the same entity as a person and can therefore be represented by a single record type (Fig. 8.7).

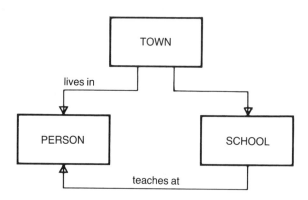

Fig. 8.7

This is not possible with a hierarchical database. IMS includes the facility to include non-hierarchical links, but it is an awkward facility and the benefits of using IMS are lost if too many non-hierarchical links are built in.

IMS, or any hierarchical database structure, is suited for applications that require very efficient access of data over a very narrow range of possible enquiries and updates.

A relational database is extremely flexible, but is not usually capable of high performance. This is because it allows for any conceivable enquiry or update to be carried out.

A network database is more flexible than a hierarchical database and less than a relational one. It tends to be capable of better performance than a relational database, although not as fast as a hierarchical one.

The CODASYL committee chose the network database as the standard for database structure. For this reason, network databases are often referred to as CODASYL databases, although the widely used network databases (IDS, IDMS, VAX-DBMS, etc.) only include a subset of the full CODASYL recommendations.

Database design

Since the most popular use of a data model is at the design stage of a database development project, it is appropriate to discuss how the database design may be based on the data model. It is not intended to cover the subject in great depth. This is because many of the techniques and considerations of database design relate to specific database management systems (DBMS), and require some knowledge of the software internals and utilities, which it is beyond the scope of this book to discuss. However, it is possible to include some general guidelines.

The obvious way to use the data model in designing a database is to copy it. Each entity type is implemented as a single record type, segment or table; each attribute is implemented as a single field or whatever; and so on. But this is often not possible within the constraints of the particular DBMS software, and even when it is possible it may not be the best solution.

Some of the more common reasons for differences between the data model and the database design are as follows. For conciseness, the terms *record* and *field* will be used for the components of the database.

Exclusion

The database may only be an implementation of part of the data model. Some attributes, entity types or classes of entity occurrence may be excluded. This may be for a number of reasons. Perhaps it is planned to add them on later. Perhaps they are being implemented on a different computer, or in some other way. Perhaps a cost/benefit study has shown that they are not worth implementing at all.

Inclusion of redundant data

It may be useful to store a piece of data more than once, or to store data that could be derived from data held elsewhere. Such duplicated or derived data is strictly redundant, and does not appear in the data model. Including redundant data in the database can make update considerably more complicated (since the database must be kept consistent) but it can make retrieval easier and quicker. Rather than read many records to calculate a total, it may be easier to read one record on which the total is stored. Indexes are usually based on redundant data, because the key of the record is held in more than one part of the file. For applications in which update is comparatively rare while retrieval is frequent, it will probably improve performance to have a judicious sprinkling of redundant data in the database.

Another benefit of including redundant data is that it allows the integrity of the database to be monitored. For example, in a network database, the key of the owner record is often duplicated in the member record so that if pointers are corrupted they can be more easily restored.

Entity split by attribute

An entity type is implemented by two or more record types: its attributes are implemented as fields of one record type or another.

For example, the entity type TEACHER may have attributes relating to formal qualifications and also attributes relating to personal circumstances. This may be implemented as two record types, a TEACHER-QUALIFICATION record and a TEACHER-PRIVATE-DATA record. Clearly both records must contain the teacher's name, or there must be some other way of relating the records together.

The possible reasons for an entity split by attribute include the following:

1 some attributes are accessed very frequently while others are accessed very infrequently;

2 some attributes are accessed by one group of users while others are accessed by another group of users;

3 some attributes require a much higher level of security or privacy than others;

4 the record would be too large unless split (which might cause physical problems with disk blocks and buffer sizes).

Entity split by occurrence

An entity type is implemented as two or more record types: the entity type is divided into subtypes, with each occurrence belonging to one subtype; each subtype is implemented as a separate record type.

For example, the entity type TEACHER may be divided into subtypes HEADTEACHER, DEPARTMENT HEAD and ASSISTANT TEACHER. Each occurrence of teacher is then represented by a record in one of the three record types.

The possible reasons for an entity split by occurrence are similar to those for a split by attribute. They include the following:

1 some classes of occurrence are accessed by different types of transactions or different groups of users;

2 there would be too many records of one type unless a split was effected (which might make the indexes unwieldy);

3 the database is being distributed over many computers in different locations.

In more complicated situations, the subtypes that are implemented as separate record types may actually overlap.

Entity merge by attribute

Two or more entity types are implemented in a single record type by combining their attributes.

This usually occurs when the entity types are closely related. Often some data are duplicated as a result of the merge, but this is considered 'cheaper' than implementing a lot of little records, where the interconnecting pointers may use more space than the actual data.

As an example, consider the problem of storing currency exchange rates. It is often easiest to solve this with a flat file, each record containing a code for the currency, the rate of exchange and the date on which the rate applied; a more elaborate structure would be unnecessary.

Entity merge by occurrence

Two or more entity types are implemented in a single record type by combining their occurrences.

For example, whereas the entity model has an entity type INVOICE and an entity type CREDIT NOTE, it may be decided to implement this as a single record type, with an extra field denoting whether a record represents an invoice or a credit note.

Dummy records

The limitations of the DBMS may make dummy records necessary, because certain structures cannot be directly implemented.

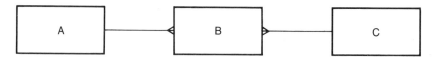

Fig. 8.8

For example, the structure in Fig. 8.8 cannot be directly implemented in a hierarchical DBMS such as IMS, which requires dummy records (known in IMS as segments) and non-hierarchical links (known as logical relationships).

A network DBMS has no difficulty with this structure, but will not be able to implement an involuted relationship without using an extra record type.

Sometimes a dummy record is required in order to implement an index or to provide sequencing.

There are many other decisions that the database designer must make. The following selective list is included for illustration only and is by no means complete.

1   Positioning of records according to frequency of use.
2   Physical representation of relationships:

       sets of pointers,
       look-up tables,
       duplications of codes and keys,
       logical relationships,
       other.

3   Index 'shape'; in other words, how many levels of index entry and what the spread is at each level.
4   Space allocation for initial set-up and subsequent expansion.
5   Procedures for overflow and expansion.
6   Hash algorithms.
7   Fixed-length versus variable-length fields.
8   Representation of numbers, dates and other small items.

Data dictionary and administration

The documentation of the data model, as described in Chapter 5, can be stored in an automated data dictionary, which is a specialized database containing data about data themselves. The data dictionary can be regarded as falling into two halves. One half concerns *real world* data, in the form of a fully documented data model. The other half concerns *computer* data, and contains full documentation of the database design. The mapping from the data model to the database design is stored in the form of cross-references from one half to the other; it is therefore possible to see exactly which parts of the data model are represented by which parts of the database.

Besides the documentation of the data structures, both real-world and computer, the data dictionary may be used to store data access models and such functional models (not described in this book) as entity life histories and data flow diagrams, together with their implementations in the form of computer procedures.

There are two administrative roles associated with data and databases. Data administration is concerned with maintaining the real-world half of the data dictionary; database administration (DBA) is concerned (among other things) with the computer half. In some companies, both roles are the responsibility of a single person or team; where these roles are separated, the data administrator is usually more senior. This is because the job of DBA is primarily technical, whereas the data administrator needs to negotiate data requirements with users, for which political skills are required.

Exercise 9

As we saw in the previous section, there is a many-to-many relationship between entities and records. An entity can be represented by many records; a record can represent many entities. Show the logical structure of a data dictionary in the form of an entity-relationship diagram.

Problems with implementing a central database

The implementation of a centralized and shared data pool is likely to cause demarcation disputes and other political problems. User departments are having 'their' data files taken away, which is bound to worry them. The data administrator must assure the users that their data are being correctly and securely handled.

Erroneously entered data have an immediate impact on other subsystems and departments that use the data. (This may be a blessing in disguise if it means that errors are noticed more quickly. Such feedback could help purify the data and ensure that necessary input controls are established and adhered to.)

Another problem in building a single central file is the interdepartment co-operation that is needed to arrive at the pertinent data elements in the file. One department may need a degree of detail which may burden the reporting source such that the quality of all input suffers. Discussions, meetings and negotiated compromise will be needed before the system can be implemented.

In a highly decentralized organization, where divisions are autonomous, the centralization of data into a central file can represent a

serious threat. The divisional managers are sceptical about the information they submit; they wonder how it is going to be used. (Perhaps they
do not want their performance figures to be known by rivals in other
divisions.) This problem has two aspects. There is first a problem of
information *security*. There is also the problem of information *validity*.
If the data administrator cannot allay the suspicions of the individual
users, that their private data will not be kept confidential, there will be
little motivation for the users to provide accurate and timely data at all.

Unless a new system satisfies the requirements of each user — both
objective and subjective (e.g. trust) — the user is obliged to maintain his
own information system, which of course defeats the purpose of the
central database.

However, it should be remembered that the implementation of a
database does not itself create these problems. On the contrary, they
are problems that always existed with the organization, underlying the
surface, which the methods of data analysis should bring to light.

Chapter 9

Management Issues

Introduction

The project leader or manager is faced with a number of problems in managing a data analysis exercise. How long should the exercise take? How should it be conducted? How should it be managed? What skills are required? What can be done to ensure success? Why does data analysis sometimes fail? Why might an exercise exceed the scheduled time? This chapter will attempt to answer some of these questions.

The aim of data analysis is to produce an unambiguous account of the organization in terms of its data. It allows everyone to agree (at a conceptual level) what the data requirements are, or at least to know the extent of their disagreement. It is highly unlikely that an organization of any size is free of inconsistency or potential conflict. Data analysis may well reveal previously hidden differences in assumptions and terminology. Resolving these differences may involve the organization in political problems. The analyst should avoid getting dragged into political fights; his only interest is that the differences are settled, one way or the other.

Scope and depth of analysis

One of the most difficult problems faced when modelling a system is knowing when to stop. There are two aspects to this problem. Firstly, that of *scope*. What is the extent of the system to be analysed? What is to be included, what left out? One must of course have a rough idea before one starts, but a precise delineation is only possible with the aid of the completed analysis itself.

To obviate presenting the sponsors of the analysis with a model of a different system from that which they had wanted analysed, it is a good idea to involve them in the analysis itself. A rough and inaccurate model can usually be produced fairly quickly. This can be shown to the sponsors in diagrammatic form, as a check that the correct areas are being covered. It can also be shown to anyone with special knowledge about the system, as a check against inaccuracy. With this feedback, the analysts can proceed to a more refined model. This is an iterative process. With careful research by the analysts and helpful criticism by all and sundry, each version of the model will be more detailed and more accurate than the previous version. This leads to the second aspect of the problem referred to above: that of *depth*. Since no model can be perfect, neither wholly accurate nor including every last detail, it would be possible to spend a lifetime polishing the model, to say nothing of incorporating changes in the real system brought about by changed circumstances. It is a management decision to take the imperfect model away from the analysts and to accept its imperfections. This may be done either on the basis of the judgement that the remaining imperfections are not important or by specifying in advance the amount of time allowed to the analysts. For an analyst to finish working on his model before he need shows deplorable lack of energy, application and/or imagination.

Building tasks and investigating tasks

There are two different types of task in a development project. Let us call them *building* tasks and *investigating* tasks.

An example of a building task is writing a program. The program is specified in advance. The project leader estimates how long the programmer ought to take. When the time has elapsed, it will be evident whether the program is finished or not. (Estimating how long something ought to take is not the same as a scientific prediction of how long something will take. It is partly an exhortation to the programmer, partly a hopeful promise to the sponsor.)

An example of an investigating task is testing a program. The objective is to discover bugs, but the bugs themselves are not specified. In a large system, it cannot be reasonably expected that all the bugs will be discovered before implementation. The objective is therefore not to discover all the bugs, but rather as many as possible.

How can a project leader know whether a program is completely tested? He cannot. All he can do is make sure the testing has been carried out as thoroughly as the time available allows.

To illustrate the difference between a building task and an investigating task, consider the reaction of the project leader when he is told that the task is finished ahead of schedule. In the case of a building task such as a program, congratulations are in order. (The purpose of program estimation is arguably to let the programmer know how hard he must work to gain the esteem of the project leader.) In the case of an investigating task, who if anyone deserves praise? If the testing is quick, can one infer the skill of the tester or of the programmer, the former for finding few bugs or the latter for producing few? Or should the project leader suspect that the testing has not been carried out as thoroughly as it could have been?

Unless given a deadline, an investigating task will continue until the participants feel they are wasting their time. Sometimes this feeling will be justified; sometimes the participants are just getting bored because of lack of motivation, although there remains plenty that could be done; sometimes a lack of imagination will lead to a shortage of ideas, although a fresh viewpoint could see many other possibilities. On the other hand, the participants may become so fascinated by the fine details of the problem that they would go on for ever trying to perfect the solution, long beyond the point where the organization stands to gain anything from further study.

The distinction between building tasks and investigating tasks is confused by the fact that building tasks can include investigating subtasks and vice versa. Writing a program may require a small investigation by the programmer to find a good way to handle the input/output efficiently. An investigating task may require the results to be published in the form of a report; report writing is a building subtask.

Just because a task is an investigating task does not mean it has to be random or undisciplined, let alone difficult to manage. An intelligent and experienced investigator, however, will know how to combine the systematic approach with the pursuing of intuitive leads. He is prepared to take short cuts, but he does not rely on there being any. He also documents the results in a standard manner.

In an investigating task, it is very important not to stray outside the terms of reference, and to cover fairly the areas inside the terms of reference. Do not get bogged down in detail in one part if it means you have to skimp somewhere else. Do not expect sympathy if you have not covered all areas in the time allocated to you.

Investigating tasks tend to be easier than building tasks to learn, although this may depend on the aptitude of the learner. It is often possible to use an investigating task as an opportunity to pass on skills. An experienced person and an inexperienced but intelligent person may be put into a team of two, and given an investigating task to work on together. A few such exercises, and the practical experience may be shared widely among the DP staff. It is even possible for end-users of computer facilities to learn to specify their own requirements in the form of a data model, after having worked with an experienced data analyst in this way.

Control of data analysis as an investigating task

A data analysis exercise is basically an investigating task (although the documenting of the data model can be regarded as a building subtask). It is therefore not appropriate to manage it as if it were a building task.

The data analysts must be given a fixed amount of time, at the end of which they are to produce a report. There can be no question of their taking any longer than the time allowed. The data analysis exercise must be carefully controlled to ensure that a correct balance is maintained between analysing items of central relevance and analysing those of marginal relevance.

During the time available, the analysts should be able to:

1   plan and schedule, arrange interviews;
2   interview users, collect sample documents and perform other fact-finding activities;
3   analyse information gathered and construct the data model;
4   clarify the revise, iron out inconsistencies;
5   document the model, write a report and present their findings.

There are at least three types of data analysis exercise. When selling, planning, estimating and controlling data analysis, it is important to know which type you are dealing with.

Initial data analysis

This is appropriate when very little is known about the area to be analysed. One or two analysts are given a fixed amount of time (from 2 – 3 weeks to 2 – 3 months) to survey the area. At the end of this survey, they should have produced a rough data model (it will by no means be perfect), a set of problem areas (usually requiring decision by management before detailed work can proceed) and a recommended schedule for further detailed study or extended study.

Detailed data analysis

After the political problems uncovered by the initial study have been settled, a detailed study would provide the information needed to design a database or other file system. The time allowed for this exercise will broadly depend on the number of entities discovered in the initial data analysis.

1 day per entity known about
+ 50–100% for auxilliary entities as yet not known about

+ 50–200% if the organization is a shambles, everybody contradicts one another, little communication between users, bad management, etc.
+ 100% if nobody is motivated to help the analysts
+ time to sort out any outstanding political problems

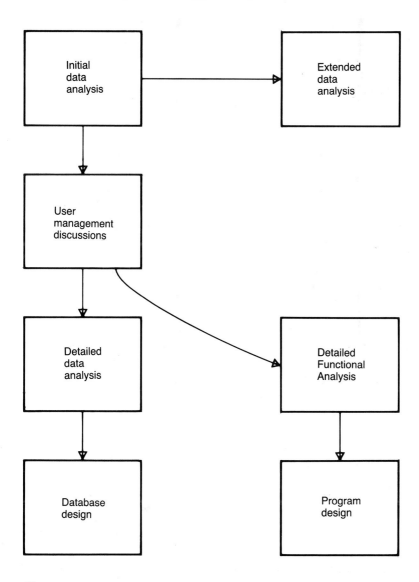

Fig. 9.1

Extended data analysis

Whereas a detailed data analysis study takes an initial data model and increases the depth of detail, an extended data analysis study increases the breadth of scope. It may turn out that it is not possible to analyse a given department or division of the organization in isolation, with a limited number of well-defined interfaces with the rest of the organization; interconnections between one area and another may be so tangled that the best approach is to carry out a much broader analysis of the whole organization, or of a larger part of it. It may even be necessary to include parts of the environment, things that do not strictly belong to the organization at all (see Fig. 9.1).

The difference between the three types of data analysis exercise can be compared to the different camera lenses used by a serious photographer. Going from an initial model to a detailed model is analogous to 'zooming in' or using a telephoto lens to eliminate irrelevant background information and concentrate on a particular area in detail. Going from an initial model to an extended model is analogous to 'zooming out' or using a wide-angle lens to obtain a broad view without focusing on individual details.

The project manager should beware of open-ended debate. All major problems, especially those with political implications, must be settled before detailed analysis and design can proceed. The user management must be made aware of the potential costs of keeping the project team idle and/or reworking and rewriting things when the users change their minds.

Dealing with problems

A data analysis exercise can encounter the following problems, as a result of which the analysts may request more time. As will be seen, there is only one case in which they should be given more time. In all other cases, the appropriate action would be to publish a report as planned, giving a full account of the problems encountered as seen by the analysts, together with their recommendations for solving them, which may include further detailed study under different circumstances or with a different brief.

Temporary unavailability of key staff

If a one-off short-term crisis hits the organization — such as illness, resignation, major business upset, etc. — then it may be advisable to postpone the exercise, with the consent of the sponsor. This should only be done if everyone is convinced that the crisis is indeed temporary.

Permanent unavailability of key staff

Some organizations totter from crisis to crisis. There may never be a time when the people who matter cannot think of some valid excuse to put off being interviewed by the analysts. It is up to senior management to insist that the day-to-day problems are put on one side for a while in order to sort out the future. If the analysts are frustrated by lack of interest, or cancelled appointments, they should not imagine this will change if they are given more time. The sponsor should be informed as soon as possible. Unless he can improve the attitudes of the key staff straight away, the exercise should be called off or a partial report published, with the possibility of trying again when the circumstances are improved.

Dissatisfaction by users

There may well be aspects of the model that cause disagreement among the users of the information modelled. It should be made clear that the report is to be regarded as a discussion document. Decisions as to information policy, strategy and priorities must be taken by senior management, although it is clearly appropriate for the data analysts to make recommendations. Political differences (and it is naive to suppose that there will not be any) can be thrashed out on the basis of the report; the data administrator may arbitrate and press for a speedy resolution of the problems, but should beware the dangers of taking sides in the boardroom battleground.

Dissatisfaction by analysts

If the analysts want to build a broader, better or more detailed data model, that is a new study, which they must persuade their bosses to sponsor.

Reasons for project failure

There are three ways in which the data analysis team and the database designers can cause a database development project to be unsuccessful. It is not always easy to apportion blame or responsibility in these three cases; the project manager should be aware of the dangers and control the data analysis and database design to avoid them.

1 It is possible to argue about data definitions until the project is no longer relevant. If the analysts are constructing a model based on their preconceptions of the problem rather than on hard information, the model is unlikely to be realistic or useful. The manager should demand that the evidence for the correctness of the model be as clearly documented as the model itself.

2 It is possible to avoid all contention by designing a structure that is so generalized that it can do anything. Difficult decisions are not made. The final system is likely to riddled with ambiguity and confusion, and to be unnecessarily expensive.

3 It is possible that a strong-willed member of the team imposes his view on his colleagues. It may be more convenient for them to accept his design than to make a fuss. The trouble with this is that the other members of the team are doing nothing. If the decision-maker is a genius, they are not required. If he is not a genius, they are not fulfilling their essential role of subjecting his model or his design to proper criticism. Inflexibilities and errors are not removed.

Of the three ways to bring a project down, the first is paradoxically the cheapest, the third is the most expensive. This is because the further the project progresses before it turns out to be on the wrong lines, the more it costs to put it right. Whereas the first cause of project failure is one in which nothing is achieved, the other two result in an incorrect system.

Reasons for project success

With every new development in computing hardware and software, the users' expectations increase. Information systems are required to be more powerful, more flexible, more 'user-friendly' and more quickly produced than ever before. The users themselves get more involved in the development of computer systems, partly by the use of prototypes, which allow the user to experience a system before it has been finally designed, and query facilities, which allow the user to formulate and carry out accesses to the database in an ad hoc manner.

Data analysis is a vital precondition for the success of these activities. Building a prototype of a data system without knowing the underlying data structure is as pointless as building a scale model of a civil engineering project without having first measured the shape of the land.

In order to build a bridge, it is a good idea to know the width of the river.

Information users are nowadays encouraged to access the database directly in order to obtain information for supporting business decisions. If their understanding of their own data structure is confused or incorrect, the information they retrieve is likely to be misleading, the decisions they make are likely to be wrong. Data analysis can help to prevent this. When the users are trained to use the computer, the training should be based on the data model (specifically on the particular user view data model). If the business decisions turn out to be incompatible with the data model, clearly action is required.

In most areas of practical work, there are two opposite dangers. One danger is to ignore common sense. The other is to rely wholly upon it. This book has attempted to steer a middle course. By following a few simple guidelines and procedures, as well as using one's head, it should be possible to obtain a clear understanding of the information requirements of a given organization. Method counts. Experience counts. Data analysis requires systematic common sense; it is at the same time quite straightforward and extremely difficult, and it is essential.

Appendix I

Normalization

Entity-relationship modelling, which is the kind of data modelling described in this book, is based on CODASYL database structures. (This does not restrict the techniques to CODASYL database development projects; they are employed by many IMS users, for example.)

A more mathematical data model has been developed by Codd and his associates at IBM, this being akin to a relational database structure. A relational data model can be *normalized;* this is a quasi-mathematical process which transforms the model into *third normal form* and thereby removes redundancy and inefficiency in the model. Techniques of normalization for entity-relationship data models are often described by analogy with those for relational data models, These techniques are then recommended to data analysts as mathematically proven, the work of Codd being cited as a reference. Many data analysts claim to carry out such normalization.

The formal techniques of normalization are not included in this book for the following reasons. (An apology is due for the fact that some of the points made here assume a familiarity with normalization. It is not worth explaining things in full.)

(1) They are not sufficient

All that normalization can do is rearrange a collection of known attributes. It is not capable of rationalizing the attributes themselves, or of discovering new attributes. Furthermore, the proponents of normalization recognize the inadequacy of third normal form by discussing the possible need for fourth, fifth and sixth normal forms.

(2) They are rarely applied rigorously

Despite the claims of the data analysts, what usually happens is that the model is informally and unsystematically checked according to a set of verbally described intuitive procedures. This is then equivalent to using some of the logical refinements described in Chapter 3. In any case, it is difficult to see how functional dependence, which has to do with the future intentions of the users, can be recognized by mathematical analysis.

(3) The analogy between the two styles is based on intuition

As far as the author knows, theoretical foundations, as have been worked out by Codd and others for relational data models, have not been produced for entity-relationship data models. This means that there is no mathematical basis for translating the techniques of normalization from one data modelling style to another.

(4) Codd's theory is itself mathematically questionable

In order that normalization be recognized as a mathematically sound set of techniques, it is necessary to find answers to some fundamental questions of mathematics.

A 'raw' data model has certain properties. The idea of normalization is to produce a data model that is equivalent to the raw data model (in some sense) but without these properties.

The procedure for normalization divides the properties to be removed into three categories. Let us call them A-properties, B-properties and C-properties. The first stage of normalization removes the A-properties only, to produce a *first normal form*.

The second stage removes the B-properties, to produce a *second normal form*.

The third stage removes the C-properties, to produce a *third normal form* (TNF).

A simple procedure would be to carry out each stage of normalization once. For this to be successful, the second stage would have to be so designed that it could not reintroduce A-properties, and the third stage such that it could not reintroduce either B-properties or A-properties.

The mathematical theory of normalization would have to prove the adequacy of the stages of the normalization procedure.

It may be the case that the stages of normalization are not adequate in this sense. Perhaps they must be applied iteratively. If any A-properties reappear in the second or third normal form, the first stage must be repeated. What needs to be proved here is that this iterative procedure is *finite*, in other words that by a successive application of the three normalization stages we always eventually reach a *normalized* data model, without any A-, B- or C-properties.

Appendix I

Is the normalization procedure determinate? If two people are set to normalize the same raw data model, will they both produce the same normalized data model? If not, will the two models be equivalent in some sense? In other branches of mathematics, it is quite acceptable to have a large set of normal forms from a given starting point, but they will usually be *isomorphic* in some precisely defined sense.

If normalization is to be accepted as a mathematically sound procedure that is useful and valid in the context of practical data analysis, more needs to be demonstrated than has yet been.

What properties of the raw data model are preserved by normalization? Are these the essential properties? Are any properties lost other than those explicitly removed? What are the consequences of the transformation in general terms?

Without satisfactory answers to such questions – which may well be hidden in the technical literature, but are certainly not widely known – it is difficult to see how mathematics can provide adequate support for the techniques of normalization.

Appendix II

Suggested Solutions to Exercises

Exercises 1 and 4 (pp. 8, 11)

Organizations	Entities	Attributes
Clearing bank	Branch	Address, Assets, Security arrangements
	Employee	Name, National Health number
	Customer account	Number, Balance
	Cash transaction	Amount, Date
Airline	Airport	Country, Name
	Route	Distance, Frequency of scheduled flights
	Aeroplane	Type, Capacity
	Flight crew	Names of staff, Shift allowance
	Passenger	Ticket number, Amount of luggage
Local education authority	School	Name, Size
	Teacher	Name, Specialized subject(s)
	Pupil	Name, Age, Form
	Exam syllabus	List of topics, Level of certificate
	Exam schedule	Timetable, Examining board
Ministry of Defence	Ally	
	Enemy	
	Warship	
	Aerodrome	
	Battalion	
	Strategy	

Exercise 2 (p. 9)

Middlesex, Spurs and Washington Redskins are occurrences of CLUB.

Ian Botham, Kevin Keegan and Roger Staubach are occurrences of
PLAYER.
Lords is an occurrence of GROUND.
Cup Final and Super Bowl are occurrences of MATCH or of TROPHY.

Exercise 3 (p. 10)

A solution to Exercise 3 is contained in diagrammatic form in the
solution to Exercise 5.

Exercise 5 (p. 13)

See Fig. A.1 for a possible E-R diagram for a sports authority.

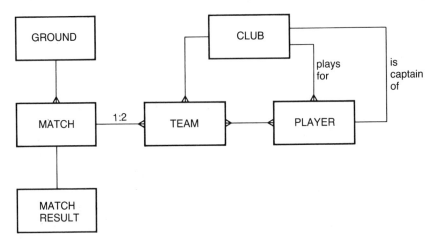

Fig. A.1

Note: because a match involves two teams, this is a special case of a
many-to-many relationship. This can be included as extra information
on the diagram.

Note: a match does not have a result until after it has been played.

Exercise 6 (p. 36)

1 A one-to-one relationship between COMPANY and ADDRESS could
represent the fact that each company has a unique head office, officially
designated for tax purposes.

2 A one-to-many relationship could represent the fact that a single company may operate many branches and in many locations.

3 A many-to-one relationship could represent the fact that a single building may house the offices of many companies, not necessarily subsidiaries of one another. This might be important to a firm in the property market.

4 A many-to-many relationship represents the most complex situation, which is a combination of **2** and **3**.

The many-to-many relationship clearly includes the other three as subsets. If this is chosen as the global model, extra attributes may need to be defined, for example to indicate at which of the many addresses the head office is located.

An alternative is to redefine the entity ADDRESS so that the name of the company is part of the full address. The many-to-many solution is then impossible, and we are left with **2**. It may be necessary to define BUILDING as a third entity type.

Exercise 7 (p. 39)

The following questions are raised by the definition of FREIGHT SHIPMENT. We may assume that definitions of CUSTOMER, DESTINATION, etc. are available.

What happens if the goods are transferred from one vessel or vehicle to another? What happens if they are stored overnight in a warehouse? Can this be regarded as a continuation of the same shipment?

What happens if the goods are processed, damaged or repackaged in transit? (Consider a shipment of rabbits!)

What happens if the goods are picked up from many locations, or are distributed to many destinations? (Consider a shipment of milk.)

This is in fact a notoriously difficult data modelling problem. Full discussion cannot be attempted without going into the operating details of shipping companies. A wholly generalized definition would have to cope with containerized shipments, tanker operations, factory ships and break-bulk, with goods ranging from tobacco to oil, from livestock to computers, and from frozen foods to academic textbooks.

Exercise 8 (p. 51)

has carried out surgery on is defined as the relationship between DOCTOR and PATIENT that holds whenever an occurrence of TREATMENT satisfies the following conditions:

1   the given patient undergoes the given treatment;
2   the given doctor is responsible for the given treatment;
3   the given treatment *is surgery*.

is surgery   is defined as the attribute of TREATMENT such that it is related via *type of treatment* to the TREATMENT TYPE named surgery.

Exercise 9 (p. 67)

A completely generalized data dictionary has a very complicated structure. The computer half must be able to include representations of any database structure.

Figure A.2 shows a very simplified data model of a data dictionary that is restricted to CODASYL databases.

The horizontal relationships, indicating which real-world objects are represented by which database objects, must be supplemented by diagonal relationships. A real-world relationship can be represented by a field or a separate record as well as by a set.

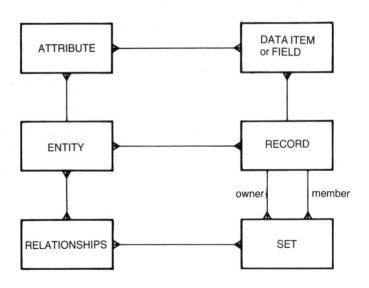

Fig. A.2

Appendix III

References and Further Reading

Codd, E.F. A relational model of data for large shared data banks, *Communications of the ACM,* **13/6** (1970).
    (The original statement of Codd's theory)

Date, C.J. *An Introduction to Database Systems* (Addison–Wesley, 1977).

Deen, S.M. The state of the art in database research, In *Proceedings of the First British National Conference on Databases, Cambridge, 1981,* eds Deen & Hammersley (Pentech Press, Plymouth, 1981).
    (A good survey of current theory, including an introduction to ANSI/SPARC architecture and comparison of data modelling ideas.)

Eden, C., Jones, S. & Sims, D. *Messing about in Problems* (Pergamon Press, 1983).
    (An interesting approach to problem solving and model building. The analyst is encouraged to adopt 'a negotiative, rather than coercive or empathetic paradigm for problem-helping'.)

Flavin, M. *Fundamental Concepts of Information Modelling* (Yourdon Press, 1981).

Martin, J. *Computer Data-Base Organization* (Prentice-Hall, 1975).

Palmer, I. *Database Systems, a Practical Reference* (CACI, 1975).
    (Although a little out-of-date, this provides a good quick introduction to databases and database theory. The author's parental loyalty towards CODASYL does not prevent him presenting its rivals fairly.)

Rock-Evans, R. & Palmer, I. *Data Analysis* (IPC Business Press [Computer Weekly], 1981).
    (An elaborate version of the Palmer methodology. Many useful insights, but with shaky theoretical foundations and confusing diagrammatic conventions.)

Senko, M.E., Altman, E.B., Astrahan, M.M. & Fehder, P.L. Data structures and accessing in data-base systems, *IBM Systems Journal* (1973), 30–94.

Senko, M.E. Data structures and accessing in data base systems past, present and future, *IBM Systems Journal* (1977), 208–257.
    (The Senko articles are two comprehensive surveys from a standpoint of IBM orthodoxy. Note the shift in IBM's terminology, from Codd's 'data bank' via 'data-base' to 'data base'. Everyone else has 'database'.)

Shave, M.J.R. Entities, functions and binary relations: steps to a conceptual schema, *Computer Journal,* **24/1** (1981).
    (An academic presentation of the Palmer methodology.)

Index

access path   47
ANSI-SPARC architecture   30, 85
attribute   7, 11, 17
  derived   24, 33f
  key   44

Bachman diagram   12
building tasks   70ff

CODASYL   47, 57, 62, 78, 84, 85
complex data access   49
computer view   30
criticism
  external   19
  internal   20ff
current system   18, 19, 32

data   4
  access model (DAM)   46ff, 67
  accuracy   39ff
  administration   67
  administrator   75
  analysis
    detailed   72
    extended   73
    initial   72
  derived   63
  dictionary   2, 32, 37, 66f, 84
  flow diagram   67
  model   2, 7ff, 14ff
    implicit   54
    relational   78ff
  ownership   41ff
  redundancy   24f, 58, 63, 64, 78
  set-up   55
  sharing   4, 28, 41, 67
  starting set   55
  storage   4
  usage   42ff
  value of   3
database
  administration   67
  design   25, 31, 37, 46, 55, 57, 63ff
  hierarchical   60

integrity   64
  network   61
  principles   57
  relational   61
  selection   54, 57
depth of detail   70, 74
derived attribute   24, 33f
derived data   63
detailed data analysis   72

entity   7, 8, 15ff
  identification   25
  life cycle   33
  life history   67
  possible   14, 17
  subtype   31, 64
entity-relationship (E-R) diagram   8, 11, 19
extended data analysis   73
external criticism   19

feature analysis   18
field   63
flat file   58
functional analysis   20, 46, 67, 73
functional dependence   23, 78

global view   30
  data model (GVDM)   28ff
grain   45

hierarchical database   60
homonym   28, 31

implicit data model   54
inaccurate information   39ff
indirect relationship   17, 20, 34
information   4
  inaccurate   39ff
  system   14, 28, 53, 76
initial data analysis   72
internal criticism   20ff

£6:50

Voluntary Controls

Voluntary
Controls

Jack Schwarz

**PUBLISHED IN ASSOCIATION
WITH ROBERT BRIGGS**

**A Dutton
Paperback**

E. P. DUTTON   NEW YORK

For information contact: E.P. Dutton, 2 Park Avenue,
New York, N.Y. 10016

Library of Congress Cataloging in Publication Data

Schwarz, Jack.
    Voluntary controls.

    1. Meditation.   2. Self-control.   I. Title.
BL627.S443   1978   248'.3   77-25347

ISBN: 0-525-47494-3

Published simultaneously in Canada by Clarke, Irwin & Company
Limited, Toronto and Vancouver

Designed by Marilyn Rey
Produced by Stuart Horowitz

10   9   8   7   6   5

Dedicated to
my parents, Magda and Bertus Schwarz
and to Gertrude and Herbert Scheller.

CONTENTS

ACKNOWLEDGMENTS

I wish to thank especially Dr. Elmer Green and his wife Alyce Green for the faith and trust they have given me during all the research we did together at the Menninger Foundation and for their continuous support.

Thanks to my editors at E.P. Dutton, Bill Whitehead and Pat Murray; to Joan Lynn Schleicher and Dick Rose for their insights and help during the pre-editing; and to Robert Briggs for making this book possible. For the illustrations I thank Eric Jungerman; for the Research at Langley Porter laboratories, Kenneth R. Pelletier; and for the fine foreword and her loving care, Gay Luce. To my partner Lois A. Scheller who seemed to be in the background, but gave lots of her time, love and patience to support me in all my work in the last ten years and also patiently helped this book to become a reality.

FOREWORD

It is particularly hard for me to write about someone I love and respect, who has taught me so much about my own attitudes, who has given me skills that I now consider my own habits of mind, and thoughts that seem to be my own along with the continual encouragement to grow. It is hard to admit that I have taken so long to recognize his depth, for Jack Schwarz is an inspired teacher in the highest sense. Because of his ability as a performer and his roles in public, I, along with his public, have taken a long time to recognize what he really is. As this book will make apparent, Jack is not just an inspired teacher with unusual powers over his nervous system and psychic gifts. He is a man of knowledge. He is also a loving and generous teacher who offers, in this book, an explanation of the methods he has used to obtain his powers. This book is a rare gift for anyone who will use it, for it holds out the keys of optimum health and a vision in which it must be clear that health and spiritual development are synonymous.

Jack is a particular inspiration to all who know him because he is the living proof of his own philosophy, and he is a model of the health he talks about. He needs only a couple of hours of sleep each night, eats sparingly, works furiously, and expresses unbounded joy and energy. His health results from an integrated and aware life, every aspect of which he takes full responsibility. He does what he advises others to do. He monitors his behavior and feelings carefully and maintains a free flow of energies by using the methods he describes in this book. During the last ten years many of his students have included doctors, nurses, and other health professionals who either attended his yearly course at the University of California, San Francisco or his many seminars and workshops. Unlike Jack, most of these health professionals have had plenty of experience being either sick or in less than optimum condition. However, they came with a sense of the limitations of the mechanistic view of the body, aware that they needed information and skills to put a more holistic view into practice. Among these audiences, Jack's scholarship in natural medicine was widely appreciated but often overstressed in relation to his spiritual knowledge.

Large groups of people were attracted by Jack's feats of voluntary control. He used to lie on a bed of nails as the preface to a talk, allowing the audience to inspect the healed punctures at the end. In a more sophisticated and scientific version of this shock procedure, he would stick a knitting needle through his forearm in laboratories at the Menninger Foundation or Langley Porter, and he would ask whether he should allow it to bleed or not while an array of sensors recorded his heart rate, brain waves, and other physiological functions. He is mentioned in many articles and books for his voluntary control of his nervous system, but the message that compelled him to attract attention is usually omitted. As a result, he has been described as an odd phenomenon and has been misunderstood and under-estimated. Those famous demonstrations were, of course, only the side effects of his spiritual knowledge and illustrate what every one of us could do if we were more in tune with ourselves.

From early childhood Jack seems to have had the self-confidence to achieve this harmony. He learned what he learned by himself. By age nine he realized that he could place his hands on a sick person who would then feel better. When Jack read of a fakir who lay on a bed of nails, he tried it for himself, undaunted by the fact that this was not what other Dutch boys of his age were doing. Living in pre-World War II Holland, he had no teachers to guide him and no long tradition to give him confirmation and support. He simply read whatever he could find in a library about these unusual phenomena and practiced for hours by himself. He discovered that he had many abilities known as psychic.

This means simply that Jack listened to his inner voices, while most of us did not. I can certainly remember "psychic" insights I had as a child, along with a sense of oneness with the natural universe—which, like so many adults, I heeded less and less as I grew older. I turned my attention from myself to the outside world, exchanging my own truth for the tools of survival, of sociability and school work. At the same age that my intuition was growing fainter, Jack was listening to himself carefully and practicing concentration. He found that he could hypnotize at a distance, intuit what people were thinking, and see auras. These powers prompted him to deeper learning. He gave to these inward studies the same energy that most of us reserve for our professions. His profession was inner knowledge, although he often held unusual jobs, such as dating antiques, to support his family. It is not the popular picture of the unfolding of a spiritual teacher. The details are too familiar to be awesome.

Jack has no church or dogma for props, no ancient tradition, no secrets, no panoply of elaborate symbolic deities. In short, he has no mystique—and we are strangely mistrustful of people whom we can understand. Because he lacks a colorful mystique and has no ancient tradition to aver his validity, his message has not received the same attention as that of a foreign guru—even though the ultimate messages are the same. The problem is that we understand his surface, his idiosyncrasies in clothing, his habit of smoking, his slight Dutch accent, the moments when he shows a little pride or ego. Jack is conducting his own process before our very eyes and sharing with us a Westerner's process of development. He lets us follow his own transformation in a way that gives hope to us all. Now that he does not have to lie on a bed of nails to win our credence, let us use the methods that he offers here for our own lives.

There is no book like this! Most men of knowledge, including the greatest masters, have not taken the trouble to lay out the steps of meditative practice so simply and explicitly that anyone—even those with no background—can learn from them to develop his own awareness. Jack is a master, and it is with enormous patience, generosity, and love that he could write this book in a way that all of us can use it. It is not a book to read through quickly, but a workbook that can have powerful effects if it is practiced in sequence over a period of months. Anyone who takes its challenge seriously is likely to begin feeling qualities that he or she may have attributed to special, "psychic" people. Moreover, anyone who practices the meditations will soon be feeling the joy of using his or her inner powers more fully, listening to his intuition, and paraconscious sensibility. Unlike many Western books on meditation, this one has been worked out and tested on more than a decade of students. Its simplicity is a testimony to Jack's patience and devotion as a teacher. It is hard to remember the beginning in detail when you are a master, and to write out the baby steps in order, after you yourself have learned to run. Still, it is the baby steps that make this book so practical.

Ten years ago, Jack introduced a group of us at a Kansas conference to some of the chakra exercises in this book. At that time, I had no background and didn't vaguely know how to relax. Inevitably I found the exercises as frustrating as they were intriguing, for I could not visualize the colors and shapes as others could. I privately assumed that I was one of those special people who couldn't do these things. Later, when I still couldn't relax much and didn't know how to concentrate, I tried to follow Jack's instructions to stimulate energy and place a cone of light around myself. Next to other people in the group, I felt sure I had experienced virtually nothing, but I followed Jack's insistence to do it my own way and practiced imagining that I could feel and see the light.

I happened to be living at the time on the upper West Side in New York City, and when I returned from the country I felt vulnerable. One evening I was walking on Broadway amidst the usual crowd of hopped-up, hyper people, junkies, and paranoids. Although I had doubted my abilities to meditate, I quickly placed a spiral of light around myself, and noticed the immediate change. In a word, confidence. Nobody trespassed into my spiral, and I was able to walk in comfort, exhilarated and interested instead of paranoid. I mention this moment because it is typical of Jack's practicality. Meditation, as he insists, is not something you do passively in a closet or corner: it is a way of bringing greater awareness, responsibility, and harmony to one's life. It is also true that it is easier to do the exercises in sequence. Unless you have been meditating a good deal, you probably won't want to skip around in this book. One problem with starting out of sequence, unless you have developed your skills, is that you may then encounter the kind of frustration I felt when I encountered one of Jack's sophisticated visualizations before I knew how to breathe and relax, not to mention, focus.

Most meditation teachers will tell you to breathe calmly, and evenly, but they rarely tell you *how*. It is invaluable to have breathing exercises laid out in detail as they are here. I found paradoxical breathing difficult at first, but it soon became enormously helpful in immediately changing my state of consciousness. Similarly, Jack's advice on sitting posture is lenient enough to allow everyone a way of being comfortable. I spent a year trying to sit in half-lotus on a round meditation pillow, and wound up with knee trouble that required an orthopedist. He turned out to have a closet full of meditation pillows from other meditation students as unused to cross-legged sitting as I. As Jack says, there is no special virtue in orthopedic troubles.

Unlike most teachers, Jack insists that you do not learn by being taught, not by following a teacher, or an authority—and not even by doing the exercises in this book precisely as they are offered. Instead, you are the active one. You must judge for yourself. If you listen carefully to yourself, you may change the exercises to fit you better, or use the information here to design your own.

The book is a tool to help you attain a deep honesty with yourself, to let go of your preconceptions and constricting self-criticisms, so that you can release your energies and your creativity. As you listen to your intuitions instead of the voices of society, you will begin to notice that your higher self can take command, and that you are on an exciting, perilous, and irresistible lifetime journey of evolution. To deny it is to choose sickness over health. To read and study this book is to take the first step in affirming your true being.

—Gay Luce

Voluntary Controls

1.

Mediating and Meditating

Meditation is a tool to help solve problems and achieve goals in our daily lives. But many people who have acquired the tool of meditation never really use it! They not only waste this valuable resource; they also run into some difficulty reconciling their daily lives with their meditative experiences. Creative meditation is an *active* form of meditation that begins as a specific practice or exercise but eventually becomes a way of life.

It is foolhardy to use any tool without becoming well acquainted with it. And this is as true of meditative techniques as it is of the proper use of a chain saw. We cannot expect to maximize its effectiveness and minimize its dangers until we learn all we can about it. The first thing to know is what the tool is used for. In this chapter, I will describe how active and passive meditation differ, how active meditation can increase our creativity, and how this practice can help maintain good health.

Practitioners of passive meditation become charged with energy by remaining quiet and receptive. Frequently, the first thing that happens as a result of this exercise is what humanistic psychologists have called *peak experiences*. These are described as experiences of bliss, joy, expanded awareness, or deep spirituality. When asked to explain how their meditating affects them, these practitioners will often respond, "I don't know exactly, but I feel great." Yet the only change in their lives is that they can occasionally exalt in the memory of the peak experience.

As they continue to meditate, less desirable phenomena begin to occur. They can become terrified by overwhelming feelings of alienation and loneliness. Visions of demons and battles with threatening forces begin to fill the world in which they first glimpsed heaven. At this point, many people begin to doubt that they are meditating correctly. If they become too doubtful or frightened, they may stop meditating. When their meditation ceases to produce appearances of someone like Jesus Christ or Krishna, disappointment and anxiety overwhelm them. The result of their efforts is that after a brief blooming, the joy of life has again disappeared. People who once walked around with their eyes raised to the sky suddenly start looking very depressed. Ask them if they are still meditating, and they will say, "No. It just doesn't work for me." If they have the courage to try it again, they usually become very fidgety. What has happened is that they have allowed all the energy to come in and to charge them up, but they have not done anything with it. The result? The bound energy affects them in a negative way, first emotionally and then physiologically.

People who are unable to integrate the negative experiences of meditation with the peak experiences have never learned what meditation really is. They have the idea that meditation will bring them closer to reality or God or that it will bring them peace of mind. But they have specific expectations about what these experiences should be. From that perspective, passive meditation becomes a form of worship, and the worshiper wants to see only the positive aspects of God. When this meditator experiences a vision of both positive and negative—the creative and the destructive cycle of the universe—he or she cannot cope with it. This problem is avoided when a meditator goes beyond a passive role and interacts with the imagery in meditation.

Creative meditation is not the receptive silence that most people expect meditation to be. Meditation is the action of becoming a mediator between opposites—between "the above and the below," cosmos and man, and positive and negative. When I meditate, I am responsible for the task of integrating everything that happens during my meditation, whether a peak experience or a traumatic one. I try to see beyond the conceptual evaluation that my reasoning mind makes for each experience, and I search for ways to apply my meditation to the situations confronting me in daily life. To meditate, then, is to be a responsible mediator.

To me, the additional *t* in the word *meditation* is an image of the tau cross, an ancient symbol of responsibility and commitment. In early Egyptian religion, neophytes were required to undergo the ordeal of being tied to the cross. This was part of the ceremony that initiated them into the mysteries of Osiris. This gesture of total commitment to the responsibility that accompanies knowledge was expected before the truth was unveiled to them. To become initiates, they had to act upon their knowledge, not just receive it. In this way, they became mediators instead of worshipers.

I am not introducing this example in order to deny the importance of worship. But I do wish to point out that there is a difference between worship by practicing the presence and worship by adoration. The first brings you into a dynamic union with what you worship; adoration keeps you separated from it. All too often, we think that being religious means that we adore God at a certain time and place and in a certain form. To me, this is as misleading as the notion that meditating is sitting passively and waiting for enlightenment.

I have found that I need to worship all the time. How? I see value in things to which I otherwise might not have given value—in the flower, the trees, the clouds, the trash can. I see value in everything and worship it because it is part of everything, but I never idolize it. I need to live God, cosmos, and universe, not separate myself by sitting, gazing, and saying hallelujah. Worship means being actively involved and interacting. We can be mediators when we worship and when we meditate. When we take this active role, we live it every moment, not just at predesignated times. Everything in life is affected, especially our health and our state of mind.

All that we feel, see, and experience in the course of life resides within us. Experiences that are absorbed but not digested form a residue that clogs our psychological functioning, much as cholesterol can block our arteries. Passive meditation stimulates the flow of energy, and when energy rushes through our psychological arteries, all the residue suddenly starts to shake loose. Consciously, we experience this as traumas that appear in all sorts of abhorrent disguises. Many guides to meditation tell us not to pay attention if these experiences occur, but if we repress these negative experiences, they will only come to the surface every time we meditate. We will come out of meditation with the memory that it was negative and the anxious expectation that the next meditation will be negative, too. The only way to stop repeating this situation is to recycle the negative material. We can diffuse the traumas by realizing that the energy bound within them can be transmuted and set free if we take an active part in meditation.

I have found that creative meditation is the method by

which to dissolve the concrete forms of negative experiences and perceive that they are the balance of the peak experiences. The two kinds of experiences constitute a whole that we must embrace if we wish to develop a balanced awareness.

Imagine a business situation in which you are suddenly overwhelmed by a problem you cannot solve. In creative meditation, you set the problem outside yourself. You are no longer personally involved. It is not *your* problem; it is *a* problem belonging to the world in which it arose. From this perspective you will be able to deal with it in a nonattached, nonemotional, nonsubjective way. Because you are no longer personally vulnerable in the situation, your reactions will be energetic and positive. Because you have become an ambassador who is aware of both the positive and the negative sides of the issue, you can bring the two together in harmony.

Creative meditation creates a focus for the neutralization and integration of all facets of your life; it is a practical tool rather than a passive state of worship. You can use it to solve problems, but it also benefits you in a more direct manner by helping you to develop a perspective on life that brings harmony to your body and mind. Better health is one of the most welcome rewards of active meditation; disease is a severe expression of repressed traumatic material. Therefore, when you interact with each experience in life as it occurs, nothing can be repressed to the extent of forming a stagnated pool of energy that finally disrupts the normal functioning of your body. By using meditation as a way of learning about ourselves, we soon come to understand how disease originates and how we can avoid it.

In the medical world today, there is an increasing interest in the so-called control of mind over body as evidenced in the literature on psychosomatic medicine. In my own experience with this phenomenon, I have found that control is a misnomer for what actually occurs when people cure themselves of headaches or undergo the remission of malignant tumors in apparently miraculous ways.

Every one of us has the capability of manifesting the power of mind over matter. But first we must understand what that power really is. It is not a force, although it does entail the flow of energy. It is unlimited, but extremely subtle. It is not control or power in the authoritarian sense; rather, it is what I call *passive volition* if you will, or, *voluntary controls*.

Passive volition is a type of will power, but its source is the kind of will we gain when we act as responsible mediators. Although I will describe this complicated concept in this chapter, passive volition must be discovered in your own experience before you can understand it fully. The techniques and ideas presented in this book are meant to help you to discover this and many other resources hidden within yourself.

When I became aware of my own ability to exercise passive volition, I used it to demonstrate to people how we can will our bodies to react to external stimuli in unusual ways. In my first years of lecturing, I would often begin a talk by lying on a bed of widely spaced nails. Then I would stand up and invite the audience to examine the punctures made in my body by the nails. Next, I would illustrate our potential to control the flow of blood by stopping or starting the bleeding from the wounds. Although the nails were never sterilized, I never suffered from an infected wound.

By this time, my audience would discard their preconceived ideas about the world and themselves; they were ready to receive new concepts. In the lecture that followed, I would try to awaken them to their creative potential and to the self-imposed restraints that prevented them from leading fuller, happier lives. I would then describe how each of us is connected to all life through our essential nature, which is spirit.

These ideas are not easy for most of us to comprehend because our attitudes have set us against any reality other than the most dense, concrete forms of energy. Only the undeniable demonstration of a fact contrary to this limited world view seems to open people's minds and hearts. After my lecture, I would again ask the audience to examine the puncture wounds because by that time the holes would have healed—or, rather, I would have willed that they would close without harm to the body.

Today audiences do not need such shock treatments to open their minds. I no longer need to demonstrate the phenomenal aspects of mind over matter except in the laboratories of scientists who are trying to understand the complexities of mind-body interactions. This new openmindedness has not come about by chance. Many demonstrations under controlled laboratory conditions paved the way. I participated in one experiment in which we monitored the physiological effects on my mind and body when I pierced my arm with a knitting needle. We were primarily checking to see whether my ability to pierce my body without feeling pain was due to blocking the experience mentally or to actually preventing traumatization of my body.

Here is the taped description of the experiment (from the film "Mind and Hand," in the C.B.C. series, "The Nature of Things," #974):

> Jack S. was asked to close his eyes and assume a meditative state. Electrodes, attached to his scalp and other areas of his skin, are monitoring a number of physical parameters. Should pain or anxiety be experienced at any point during this demonstration, a rapid change in meter readings would be expected. Jack is completely on his own and is receiving no bio-feedback information.
>
> From being in a range of above 13 cps, the record is

now showing a gradual increase in alpha frequency. As a demonstration of the voluntary control of a state of pain, we are going to ask Jack to place a large-diameter, 24 to 26 gauge steel, unsterilized knitting needle completely through his left bicep. An important factor to note here is that there has been no prior preparation, and that Jack is not in any hypnotic state. Jack says, "I'm going to puncture the arm with this needle. I have no specific place to do this, but will insert it right about here, and push it through so that it comes out on the other side. Now it is totally through the arm."

A flashing red light shows no change in heart rate; no change is recorded in skin temperature. The EEG record shows no indication of stress of any kind. Despite the fact that the needle was inserted right through the arm, Jack S. is also able mentally to stop any bleeding that would normally have taken place. The small marks left by the needle heal very rapidly. This is mind over matter to a highly significant degree.

In this experiment, carried out at Langley Porter Neuropsychiatric Institute in San Francisco with Dr. Kenneth Pelletier, each physiological test was followed by an interview in which I was asked how I had felt and what I had thought as I did the experiment. After the needle test, I said:

Since I know that I'm going to insert the needle, there's no need for pain. I've brought myself into a state of non-attachment, which means that I keep my attention occupied by visualizing something outside my being, paying no attention to my arm. In this way it can be said that I'm not putting the needle through *my* arm; I'm putting the needle through *an* arm. . . . My body has agreed that this may happen, and no fear, no pain will be felt. Because I

am non-attached and accepting, I do not feel threatened
by the strange event occurring.

The abilities that I demonstrated in these experiments are
within everyone's reach. When there is a condition of harmonious interaction between your mind and your body, you
can practice passive volition. To attain such harmony, you
need to develop a nonattached point of view, an awareness of
the purpose of life, and a flow of energy or consciousness that
is not hindered by fear or repressed emotion.

Creative meditation is an accessible and effective tool for
this task. In the chapters that follow, I will delineate many of
the meditative techniques and other aids that encourage and
implement harmony between mind and body. This book can
serve as a catalog of tools. However, they are valuable only if
they can stimulate you to become a mediator in life and to
develop your own meditative methods. Think of my techniques as building blocks. Select some, and combine them
with others to suit your own needs. If you can be creative with
these exercises rather than blindly replicate them, this book
can become a manual for your own life. By using it as a guide,
you can find your way to health, creativity, and dynamic interaction with the universe around you.

2.

Self-Initiation

In this chapter, I will describe some of the practical but more esoteric and theoretical foundations of creative meditation as a means for self-initiation. All the exercises included in this book will help you to develop the ability to analyze yourself creatively. They require that you use all your perceptual faculties. As you practice, you will learn to credit information from your intuitive sense with the same certainty that you grant the perceptions of your physical sense organs. Your powers of perception will intensify, and as they do, they will make you as aware of your inner experiences as you are of your outer environment. Many times, students have asked me why their meditation seems devoid of the fascinating images or provocative realizations that other meditators claim to experience. Are such insights really only rare occurrences? My response is that not only is this inner vision available to everyone who practices meditation but also it is active all the time, not just during meditation. We have not learned how to turn our attention to the inner world because we spend most of our lives focusing on mundane matters in the outer world. Creative meditation teaches us to redirect our attention so that we can live in both worlds. When we have learned to live in this way, nothing is hidden. We can become aware of all the attachments and fears that hinder us, as well as of the inner resources that can help us. Through that awareness, we gain greater confidence in our ability to meet the demands of our lives successfully and to understand how we are learning and evolving.

Use the techniques of creative meditation to make you aware of your progressive evolution, the irreversible growth that occurs when you gain knowledge through experience. When you consciously experience something, an abstract concept becomes manifest. For example, if you are afraid but repress your fear, it is preserved within you. But if you become conscious of it and experience it directly, you can interact with it. When you activate it, you are released from it by learning from the experience. A productive type of meditation such as creative meditation stimulates this process.

A perfect act is a physical expression of the mental manifestation of spiritual integration. Unless the integration is carried through to the physical level, it will simply be an unfertilized seed. It is very easy to become attached to our insights and visions. Very often, we do not realize that a revelation is not the apex of experience but just the seed that needs to mature by being allowed to grow into a perfect act. Insights are the mental manifestation of truth. These experiences should be transformed into actions. Do not fear an insight; have faith in it and act upon it. Never consciously control it; let it ripen and express itself in the ways in which you react and act in your life. The active expression of truth is the purpose of life. So use meditation to develop awareness of your evolution toward this goal.

In order to achieve this ability, meditation should first be used to balance our physical, mental, and spiritual states. Therefore, the exercises in this book begin with methods for calming body and mind so that they support the meditative state. These preparatory instructions are followed by discussions of the visualization exercise, or reverie, and the complete creative meditation cycle. One of the applications of these techniques is then demonstrated in Chapter 6, "Health and Human Energies." Many philosophic and meditative traditions state that certain areas of the body are the physiological centers of energy and that blockage in these centers creates disease. Conversely, when you achieve the proper flow of energy, you have taken a major evolutionary step. The final group of exercises (in Chapter 7) will present techniques for the activation and regulation of energy flow through these centers, commonly called *chakras*.

Activating the chakras, awakening our intuitive powers through meditation, and seeking an integration of mind, body, and spirit were once the exclusive province of the shaman and the mystic. Today they can be fairly common goals; certainly, the means of attaining them are available to everyone. We need not undergo the ritualized ordeals that ancient initiates experienced in order to gain knowledge. Rather, we need to awaken to the fact that we are *all* initiates.

How do we become initiated? By our own change of consciousness. I do not need another individual to shower rose petals over me and say, "You are now initiated." Once I have the initiative to take responsibility for my own consciousness and start working with it, I *become* an initiate. However, I am an initiate at the lowest level of discovery, and I may yet experience many initiations. I know that I can achieve these initiations only by continuing to move beyond the level at which I am competent. Every time I discover another plane of consciousness, I will become an adept in that plane. If a doctor examines only one organ of a patient, with no involvement with the patient's mind or the rest of his body, he will never know the whole man nor be able to heal him properly. He is an initiate only to that part. I want to be initiated into the part, the whole body, and other bodies as well. By moving into the unknown, I gain the opportunity to expand my competency. This is one reason why we should remain nonattached to any single aspect of ourselves or our lives. We must learn to let it go so that we can grow.

Today many people are becoming aware of the fact that no one can take the initiative for them. They cannot rely on others, on society, or on fate to bring them the fulfillment they desire. They have finally realized that the only consolation and understanding that can be gained are to be found within themselves.

Metaphysicians tell us that we are now experiencing a turning point for humanity. The common expression for this is that this is the Aquarian age and that in it we have the opportunity to move to a new level of consciousness. The turmoil we feel within ourselves and see in the world around us results from the pressure to change, the challenge offered by the new age.

Part of this challenge is that we should assume the responsibility of becoming our own authority. If we start to heed the teachings of the wise men of the past, we should remember this. Jesus Christ, one of the initiates whose voice is still heard, said, "Ye can do the things I do and greater things will ye do." As long as we keep worshiping the man without living his principles, we cannot even begin to do the things He did. And what about the still greater things we could do if we really understood His principles? In my view, we should not be striving to follow *an* individual. We should understand that the teachings of all wise people are tools for us to find our own ways to becoming initiates.

I want to reiterate the importance of the relationship between taking an active role in your meditation and becoming a cocreator in your life. Being a cocreator means that you are the final authority on what is true; but this cannot happen until you have enough faith in yourself to take that responsi-

bility. Whenever you become a student or try to teach someone else what you know, it is helpful to remember this.

It is particularly necessary to keep this in mind when you
learn methods of meditation or of any other self-actualizing
technique. For example, the main source for this book is my
own meditation experience. The ideas and practices are particularly suited to me but not necessarily to anyone else. Never-
theless, they can stimulate you and direct you to develop
your own.

I have found that many of the experiences I have had are
confirmed in the philosophy or the stories of other meditators.
I am often asked, "What is your philosophy?" I reply, "I have
a philosophy of my own which is similar in many ways to
many other philosophies." The meaning of the word *philosophy* (Gk. *philo,* love; *sophia,* wisdom) is love of wisdom. If you
have wisdom, you know yourself, and therefore you can create
your own philosophy.

Those who cannot find their own philosophy through
meditation must adhere to another's. In the process, what
began as a dynamic expression of wisdom for one person becomes a static belief system. The passive followers of philosophies and religions can only know what is written about them.
Their knowledge is based on belief, not personal experience.
And personal experience is the only way to gain wisdom. It is
also the only way to know something without a shadow of a
doubt. By living it, you know it firsthand. When many people
say, "I have faith," they mean, "I believe." When I say I have
faith, I mean, "I know it because I have experienced it, even
though I may not have experienced it in the concrete world."
I have experienced it during meditation in a state that
transcends the perceptual world. This experience became a
conscious part of me, something so clear that I do not hesitate
to express it in the concrete perceptual reality of the physical
world as well.

Experience then becomes knowledge that can be communicated, and that is what I am describing in this book. It is like having a good investment and knowing there is someone backing you up. You can't go wrong. But when I follow the authority of some other person or teaching, I can go wrong every time because the authority might fail me when applied to the reality of my own life. Therefore, I am an eclectic, not because I have followed many philosophies, but because I have observed many philosophies. I can say, "Yes, this is what I have experienced. Thank you. That confirms what I am doing."

It is very helpful, then, to read books and listen to others in order to find ways to express your experiences. All the spiritual teachings are useful; none should be excluded. The truth lies within all of them, but not all of us can peel the egg and find the truth within.

In my classes a new student will say, "Right. You were talking about Christian Science." Another says, "Right. You must be a Sufi." "Right. That's what the Zen Buddhist says." "Right. That's real Christian teaching." All these people want to make me an authority in order to hear my teachings. But they misunderstand. Neither my classes nor this book are meant to be authorities. They are an assembly of my own peak experiences and a description of the methods I used that produced these peak experiences.

Before practicing the techniques of creative meditation, it is important that you adjust your attitudes toward student-teacher roles: Realize that you cannot learn by being taught. We misunderstand the role of the teacher. Teaching should mean sharing our experience with other people because we feel a deep desire that others may experience it themselves and share it with us. It is a process of exchange, a transference of thoughts without dogmatizing. Their experience may be different from ours, just as the seed is different from the flower. A teacher can share experiences as if sowing seeds so that others can grow their own flowers. In teaching, one should only say, "Here is a model. If you like the model, perhaps you would like to know how it was formed. Let me give you the method. I am handing out patterns. So here is a pattern. Use my pattern if you like it. You like my dress? You like my suit? If you don't like the pocket on the back, you can put it in front—wherever you like. And if you want to put it on the top of your collar, that's okay with me, too."

Many teachers teach their students to play follow-the-leader, and that often holds the students back from self-discovery. The teacher who gives us information and molds our minds by telling us what is true and what is false is really practicing behavior modification, not education. We trust the teacher more than we trust ourselves and blindly say to ourselves, "If the teacher does it, it must be so."

Today there are many gurus whose students copy everything they do. The guru may tell them to find their own inner wisdom, but in the next sentence, he intones, "Now, my children, let us meditate." By saying that, he assumes the authority of a parent, looking upon his students as children, not as peers. But students *are* their teachers' peers.

We seek teachers because they have experienced things we have not yet known but wish to know. Should the fact that they have had the opportunity to experience those things before we have make them absolute authorities over us? Imagine a neighborhood in which the children are still playing with tricycles. Suddenly one of them gets a bicycle. This child becomes the authority on bicycles until everyone else gets one. Then they realize, "He didn't know that much about bicycles. As a matter of fact, he's not that good at bicycling at all!" As long as the other children had not experienced bicycling, they looked up to this glossy chrome thing and the lucky child who proudly rode it. And the child on the bicycle looked down his nose at them.

Who are we to be authorities over other people? Certainly, we need teachers throughout our lives. I have had a thousand gurus, but not one of them taught me anything. Indeed, they *confirmed* me. Every time I saw my own experience reflected in the words or actions of another person, my own authority was confirmed. From each of the many books I have read, I have extracted the material relevant to my own needs and perspectives and dismissed the rest. Every one of them has confirmed me, sometimes with only one sentence. This is the important thing. All my gurus have enabled me to realize that I am not the only one who is envisioning the world in a certain way. But they have also helped me to understand that the model created by all my perceptions is unique to me. That model is important to others only when it encourages them to make their own models.

What will people do with the experiences they have if they take this book seriously and practice the exercises? Will they say, "This is Jack Schwarz's method"? No. If they have followed the instructions carefully, they will be developing their own methods. There are an infinite number of pathways. The teacher should merely hand out maps. Each of us must travel the map by creating our own pathways. Suppose that I ask, "How do you get from San Francisco to Seattle?" One person might say, "I go by way of Sacramento." Another might respond, "I go by way of Chicago." The first person may think that it is unnecessary to go to Chicago en route to San Francisco until the second person explains, "Before I go to San Francisco, I must attend a meeting in Chicago that will determine what is to be done when I arrive in San Francisco."

Each of us has his or her own path to travel and his or her own reasons for the journey, but we all will encounter milestones that look familiar because they have been seen by others. Their descriptions are like travel guides we read before going on a trip. It is like seeing a picture of a temple in

Malaysia. We can all share that picture, but we will each have different experiences if we go there. Only then will we know about the sweet-smelling fruit market in the square outside the temple. Some of us might meet the people there and learn about the temple ceremonies. Although the temple looked the same to us all in the picture, it differed for each of us when we encountered it.

There is only one truth, but there are many different ways to experience it. They may be similar, but they are never exactly the same. That is why we are often dissatisfied when someone describes an experience that we have had ourselves. In my classes, people sometimes say that according to their experiences, I have omitted important aspects of a topic or that I have exaggerated others. That is because it is impossible to use the terms of this three-dimensional world to describe a multidimensional perception that is experienced during meditation or insight. That is what makes everything unique.

When we understand this, we realize we must respond to questions by saying, "Go there, and experience it, but do not ask me exactly how it is." You want to say more, but you cannot. You can describe the experience, but you cannot recreate it for someone else. You can only awaken them to its existence. Sometimes if you do describe an experience, another person might get the feeling of it. But you must still advise them not to be satisfied with that feeling alone. Then they will not make society's mistake of allowing religion and philosophy to become dogmatic.

Our responsibility as teachers is to share what we have freely. Our responsibility as students is to choose our teachers and select what we need from what they say, rather than making them into dictators, idols, or gods.

A good model of this kind of educational process can be seen in the Sufi tradition of the Middle East. The Sufis will invite novices and strangers to their most sacred ceremonies and reveal to them their most sacred teachings because, as they say, those who cannot hear, will not hear. On the other hand, if the stranger turns out to be someone who has already initiated himself, they will be very glad to share their wisdom with such a person—and learn from him as well.

This is a principle I try to follow. I am quite convinced that when I am standing in front of my students, there might be many masters among them. At that moment, they may never have brought their mastery into action, but maybe I am that little spark that can activate them. I guarantee you that if they all could stand up and proclaim their mastery, if they could show me that in their actions and in their lives they can practice their wisdom, I would be glad to sit down and listen. My job would be finished. You see, I am trying to work myself *out* of a job, not into one. I do not mind becoming an apprentice again.

The exercises and information I have collected are presented here to encourage you to awaken to your own mastery. If you practice these exercises and allow your intuition to give you your own adaption of them, you will find the teacher you seek. If practiced and adapted to your individual needs, they can help you begin to become aware of the self—not just the physical self, for we are more than just a physical form. We have a mind and substance and a source from which we derive our being. Then you can become aware of this world by developing what I call *universal peripheral vision.* You will expand your vision until you begin to perceive much more than you do now. You will perceive with both your physical eyes and your spiritual understanding. Finally, you can begin to express this awareness in all your actions, to practice it in every thought and deed. The challenge of our age is to become alchemists, transmuting the energy of insight and wisdom into practical living and thus to manifest the divine on earth.

3.

Preparing to Practice

What happens to our consciousness when we meditate? We seem to gain a perspective on our experience that is expanded beyond normal awareness. Unless we understand how our minds can operate in this way, it is difficult to feel comfortable with meditative experiences and to apply meditative techniques to daily problems. Therefore, before describing creative meditation techniques that help us to attain this expanded perspective, I will introduce you to the part of the mind that is the hidden source of creativity and intuition.

THE PARACONSCIOUS MIND

Most of us have been educated to live according to the process of logical verification. Our attention has been diverted from the process of self-discovery. We say that we "know" something, but actual knowing comprises three functions: thinking, feeling, and knowing. *Thinking* is based on a logical verification of sensory perceptions, identifying them with the aid of preconceived concepts. *Feeling* is our emotional feedback and responses to the external world. *Knowing,* however, is based on intuitional experience.

Intuitions are the result of a process of creative discovery that occurs within us. Normally, we are unconscious of the process and only consciously perceive its culmination when we intuit an answer or gain insight into a problem. Many people are uncomfortable when they have to admit that they cannot explain how their insights arise. They know *that* they know, but they do not know *how.*

Each of the modes of discovery—thinking, feeling, and knowing—are functions of different aspects of the mind. Respectively, these are the conscious mind, the subconscious mind, and the superconscious, or what I call *paraconscious,* mind. Becoming aware of the paraconscious mind is one of the goals of meditation.

The awareness we gain by means of intuition arising from the paraconscious mind is difficult to describe because it is not derived from or limited by our sensory apparatus. Let me give you an analogy. Imagine that we are individual drops of water in the ocean. Each water drop reverberates in response to everything else that happens in the ocean because every slight movement is transmitted, in varying degrees, to all parts of the ocean. The wholeness that is the cosmic ocean can be called the *universal mind.* This omniscient mind is individualized within us as our paraconscious mind, and it is through this aspect of our mind that we partake of all-knowingness. When we understand this, we have become aware of the nature of intuition. Its source is that knowingness which is beyond both the subconscious and the conscious mind. Intuitions are our momentary awareness of the fact that all of us are in constant, perpetual connection with the total universe, with God. Such moments are unusual, and most of our perceptions arise from another process in which we consciously evaluate our experiences and rationally verify them.

Our daily experiences make sense to us because we have been taught to impose a structure of time and a causal sequence upon them; one thing follows after another and is the result of what has gone before. We verify these patterns by using logic. However, there are three limitations to this mode of perception: First, we are imposing a preexisting cognitive structure on what we perceive. Second, our perceptions are limited to our grosser senses because intuition cannot be derived from logical reasoning. Third, the cognitive structures that we apply are not our own; we use a language and an understanding of logical principles that have been created by long-term social consensus.

Preconceived evaluations blind us and limit our experiences to what we already know. If we wish to learn and grow, we need to remove all the restraints on our perceptions. Most binding of all are the closed doors to the paraconscious mind. I would like to see each individual acknowledge the perceptions of the paraconscious. That is the way to discover the creative source within us and to learn to rely on our insights rather than on the discoveries and authority of others.

The most common avenue to inner discovery is through the world of dreams. Ancient societies and so-called primitive peoples have all appreciated the significance of dreams. They realized that dreams reveal and verify inner conditions and awarenesses that are often hidden to the rational, conscious mind. I am not suggesting that dreams give us a better picture of reality than our normal waking consciousness provides, but they do provide additional information that can enhance our awareness. They allow us to experience the perceptions of the subtle senses of the paraconscious mind.

These perceptions can be integrated into our day-to-day lives and can help us to solve problems and find more meaning in our activities. For example, inventors will tell you that they require both logical reason and creative intuition to make something that has never been made before. They have an idea and consciously work it out until they reach an impasse, a place beyond which their rational mind cannot go. The inventor of the chemical model of proteins had schematized most of it by applying and adapting the laws of science and logic, but he was unable to complete it. No matter how he analyzed the problem, he could find no solution. One morning he remembered, to his great frustration, that he had dreamed the solution and forgotten it as he awoke. So he said to himself, "When I sleep tonight, I will dream of the solution again, but this time I will wake up immediately and write it down." He went to bed, and again his dream solution confronted him. He woke, scribbled it down, and fell back to sleep. The next morning he was very pleased and surprised to find his sketch, for he had forgotten the dream once again.

One of the first things we learn when we pay attention to the quiet voice of the paraconscious mind is that as soon as a problem arises, the solution is born. The problem appears before the conscious mind while the solution hides in the unconscious mind. Through the paraconscious mind, we can *know* the solution as soon as we encounter the problem. Without such insight, we spend our energies pursuing the problem and finally becoming identified with it. Although we may declare that we are looking for a solution, we are actually hanging onto the problem and not allowing it to transform itself into its alter ego, the solution.

Once you learn to listen to your inner voice, your paraconscious mind can become a terrific problem solver. Your dreams can be an effective means to this end. Present the problem that has frozen in your conscious mind to your paraconscious by making the *decision* to dream about it. If you want to hear the answer, you must first ask for it.

Our lives seem to revolve in a cycle of problems and solutions. The most radical expression of this cycle can be experienced when we understand that every time we sleep, dream, daydream, or have an inspiration, we *die!* Part of us fades away and never returns. In its place is an area of new growth evolved from what we *were*. The voice of the para-conscious is the sound of both destruction and creation, and it can be amplified by creative meditation.

I meditate every night. I do not set an exact time for it, but I know that I will meditate. The best time for me is usually an hour and a half to two hours before I go to bed. What is my motive for meditation? I want to die—to die out of my present state and to discover new aspects of me that are evolving. I do not want to hinder this growth or become stagnant. And I want to observe this growth.

You should never fear that you are not growing. You *are*. What might not be growing is your awareness of growth. When you are unaware of something, you cannot express it. You cannot practice the new you. Your daily death and rebirth are easier to live with when you experience them consciously every day. We are constantly passing into new stages, and we should be prepared to deal with them, to live in them and not be surprised or frightened by them. When we repress our awareness of growth and refuse to change, a pressure within us increases until we are finally forced to acknowledge it. Often the pressure expresses itself as disease. Meditation offers a bridge to walk consciously from one stage of growth to the next.

People often speak of mind and body as if they were two different and separate entities. Body and mind can never be separated during this physical episode of our existence. Recall for a moment what you have seen of water transformed into snow. Could there be snow without water? Without the substance of water, there would be no snow. Snow is only a form into which water can be transformed. Our individual minds, then (here we speak of the whole mind, not of any particular part or division), are like water that is transformed into snow.

The universal mind (water), which is impersonal, becomes individualized (crystallized, like snow) within us as personal minds.

Spirit is the prime substance from which everything is made. This is why I believe that our individualized minds created our bodies. Our bodies are contained within our minds, not the reverse. Mind thoroughly penetrates every cell of our physical bodies. Scientists have partially realized this in their discovery of the chemicals RNA and DNA, which are nutrifying chemicals and which communicate energy between the brain and all the other cells. Thus, all your life, each cell has contained right in it the memory pattern of your total being. And just as DNA and RNA are immanent and complete in every cell, the universal paraconscious mind is immanent and complete in each of us. We may have forgotten it, we may have insulted it by neglect, but it is still there, permeating our beings.

The body is actually mental because mind is the manifester of spirit substance. We are tripartite beings comprised of spirit, the essential substance; mind, the manifester; and body, the expresser. When these three parts harmonize by being entirely operative and interactive, we experience growth and allow it to happen with full awareness. The first step toward this integration occurs when we open the doors of the paraconscious mind and let intuition flow into our consciousness.

Let me illustrate this point by describing Pascal's law of communicating vessels (see Figure 1). If there are three vessels connected to one another, when fluid is poured into one, it will flow and fill all three equally, no matter what their individual shape or size. However, if surface pressure is applied to one of the vessels, the flow will be blocked.

In human terms, pressure can be equated with trauma, fear, and repression. Most of this kind of pressure is produced

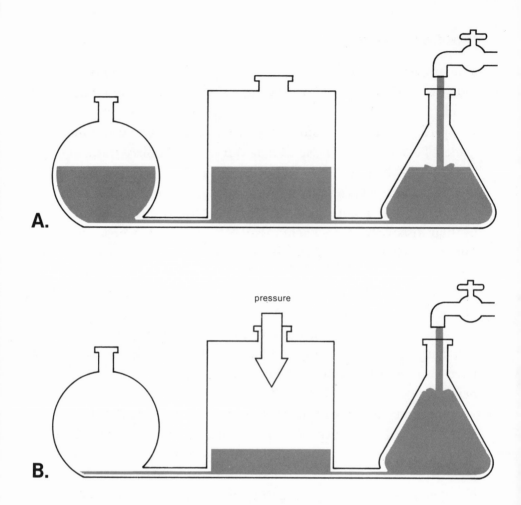

Fig. 1. Pascal's Law of Communicating Vessels

and stored in the subconscious mind. The subconscious is the passageway by which the flow of intuitive energy from the paraconscious reaches awareness. When this intermediary aspect of mind is pressured, our inspirational source is closed to us.

It is precisely in the paraconscious domain that we grow; successive waves of intuition accumulate there until their energy demands that they be brought to the surface, acknowledged, and consciously absorbed so that the growth of the entire organism can be consistent. We need to learn to give the conscious mind the capacity and the opportunity to accept intuition. But as it is, we have allowed this input to remain in the paraconscious mind and hindered it from filtering up to our consciousness.

It is like living in a three-room house in which you have piled all the furniture into the living room and kitchen and blocked the door to the bedroom. For the rest of your life, you are doomed to sleep on the couch while the cozy bedroom stands empty!

Figure 2 summarizes the dynamics of the mind. *A* is the central, conscious mind. It is the consciousness experienced in the normal waking state. As the expressive reasoning center, it is the result of the integration of all internal processes. It determines how we appear to the world.

B is the subconscious mind, which coordinates the physiological activity of the body. In particular, it directs most of the reflexive bodily functions. The *voluntary control of internal states,* a term frequently used today, refers to the ability to become aware of these unconscious functions. When you can focus your attention on these subtle physical processes, you can correct debilitating reactions such as the physical effects of hypertension, stress, and anxiety.

The subconscious mind has a second function: the development and expression of dreams. These include dreams that arise to solve problems, dreams that are premonitional, and dreams in which we experience the otherwise-repressed contents of the unconscious—phobias, traumas, obsessions, paranoid delusions, as well as desires and needs.

The subconscious mind also functions as the archives or library. All the perceptions the organism receives (from whatever sources) are registered here, with the new piled on top of the old. Perceptions are slowly absorbed by the memory, which

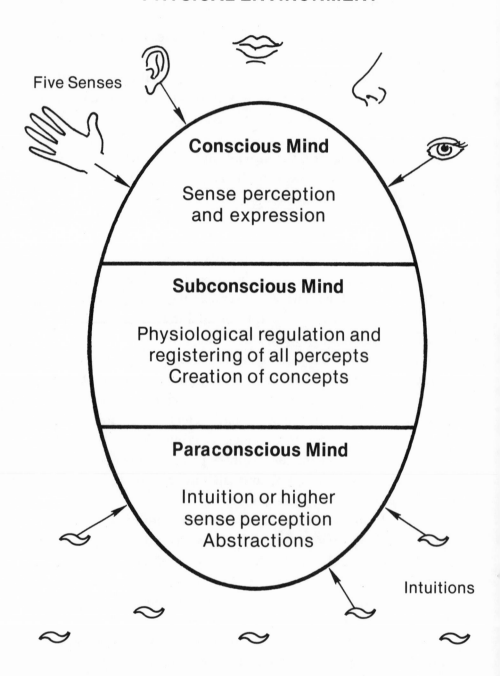

PHYSICAL ENVIRONMENT

Five Senses

Conscious Mind

Sense perception
and expression

Subconscious Mind

Physiological regulation and
registering of all percepts
Creation of concepts

Paraconscious Mind

Intuition or higher
sense perception
Abstractions

Intuitions

UNIVERSAL ENVIRONMENT

Fig. 2. A Diagram of Mind

files them away according to a number of learned patterns. This filing process categorizes percepts, thus converting them into concepts that can be retained over time and retrieved when information about a certain category is required. When our reactions to situations are entirely governed by these archives, we behave like robots, closed down and limited in our experiences. In order to interact, rather than merely react, concept should be used to balance percept. Without overwhelming and nullifying our present experience, concepts can be used to sharpen our understanding and evaluation of it.

C is the paraconscious mind. This aspect is neither subconscious nor conscious; it is supraconscious. Our physical sense organs perceive the gross manifestations of energy (i.e., matter), and the percepts of these sensations are received by the subconscious mind (*B*). But there are less dense aspects of the universe, subtle energies that carry a different kind of information to us. They bring us the message of the nature of the whole; whereas our physical senses inform us only about the parts. Paraconscious mind partakes of the omniscience of universal mind. When the paraconscious is clogged through our lack of creative expression and our denial of our intuitions, we suffer from imbalance. We are dynamic beings, just as the universe itself is a dynamic process, and any restriction of the flow of energies causes strain and tension. These eventually lead to breakdown, manifested as disease, trauma, catastrophe. This is the enforced change that results from resistance to change. Whether we are talking about galaxies or individual human beings, the process is the same.

When we allow the flow of energy to go from the paraconscious to the subconscious mind, the flow regulates the positive or negative charges attached to stored concepts. Then concepts are illuminated by creative intuition, and our actions and thoughts are potentialized by new insight.

The exercises in dreams and reveries given in Chapter 4 are meant to help you become familiar with the paraconscious mind and its patterns of operation. These are the media of the paraconscious mind. Using creative meditation, you can learn to interact with the paraconscious mind; then you will begin to direct your rational mind to implement the intuition provided by the paraconscious.

ATTITUDES

We have investigated the aspect of our minds that meditation teaches us to activate and add to our available resources. Now we can list the mental attitudes that are conducive to the activation of the flow of insight from the paraconscious mind. All these reminders will be restated and elaborated later in the book when they are described as parts of the meditative process. Here we introduce them to serve as orientation guides rather than as specific practices.

MONITOR YOURSELF

During all the exercises in this book, your attitude should be that of a passive spectator, one who merely observes what the body and emotions are doing. The information you will receive from self-observation breaks the cycle of dependence on other people's expectations of what you are supposed to be. It releases you from the anxiety inherent in accepting outside goals and demands. In self-observation, you use your own eyes to look at yourself as you are, without expectations or preconceptions. To do this in your daily life is to take a step forward toward responsible freedom and growth. In meditation, self-observation plays an essential role.

One of the techniques to use to optimize the powers of self-observation in meditation is the creation of a mirror image of yourself, a second you. This is a way of encouraging a state of nonattachment, so that you will not cling to a certain identity and will be free to allow the mirror image full liberty in its behavior. The unconscious and paraconscious can then reveal themselves through this mirror image.

TAKE RESPONSIBILITY

Through self-observation, you can learn to tailor techniques of meditation to your own special needs and abilities. The first time you carry out the directions for breathing, reverie, and creative meditation, follow the given pattern. If you are watching yourself inside and out, you will note any resistance that your mind, your emotions, or your body has to these patterns. Note this reaction. When you have completed the exercise, consider why there was any resistance. Quite often you will resist because there is a more appropriate procedure for you to follow. Your unconscious is informing you that for you there are better modes of self-discovery than the ones I am suggesting.

What do you do in that case? The next time you begin the breathing exercise, for example, adapt my method according to what has been indicated by your unconscious, to what "feels right." Do not do the exercise as I have told you (or as anybody else may tell you); do it as you are telling yourself. Do not get stuck in my methods; do not let them dominate you. Adapting methods to your own needs is harder than you may realize because it takes courage and responsibility to do so. You must consciously take up the task of self-awareness and leave me or any outside authority behind you. It is much easier to be a good technician and learn a variety of methods and techniques, but that will not get you to your goal of self-discovery.

The first step in self-responsibility is to loosen the rigid control that the conscious mind usually exercises over your organism. This is the major value in beginning meditation with breath control, for breathing is the autonómic process most accessible to voluntary manipulation. After you become accustomed to paradoxical breathing (see "Breathing Patterns" in Chapter 4) and impose this pattern on your breathing mechanism, then *let go!* Stop watching your breathing, and let the wisdom of your body determine the pattern of your breath while you pay attention to the next phases of the creative meditation cycle.

To be responsible for yourself, you must be able to trust yourself. When you know your inner world as well as you know your face in the mirror, you will gain this trust in your intuitive or preconceptual knowledge. The process of inner discovery brings what was unconscious into awareness, shining light upon it and then letting it recede from your vision again. It is a cycle of concentration and relaxation. Remember that you are not trying to exercise mental discipline over all your actions, reactions, and decisions. Your goal is to become open to and aware of *all* the information and experiences of your organism.

You can gain this awareness only by encouraging it, by paying attention to its earliest subtle appearances. Learn the techniques in this book for the purpose of coaxing your own adaptations or new methods into existence. And do not think that the process stops when you have created a personal meditation cycle. As you become adept at your practices, they will no longer be as provocative of growth as they were when you struggled with them. As you evolve, so should the practices and exercises that you use to help you grow. Do not become rigidly attached to any method, even your own. Enjoy the new, more challenging techniques that will be suggested by the paraconscious mind in the form of intuitions.

BECOME A TRANSMITTER

During meditation, we need to be relaxed and still. We do not want to put the entire mind and body to rest, only the conscious mind that dominates awareness. When the body has been quieted by the use of breath control and relaxation techniques and the conscious mind no longer interferes, the paraconscious and unconscious can be experienced.

Many people cannot achieve this stillness, despite their sincere efforts to do so. As soon as they begin to meditate, they become very restless. Their bodies and trains of thought constantly interfere with their concentration. I tell such people to stop meditating for a while. What has happened is that they have too much energy stored up. They have passively meditated without using the energy from meditation to be creative and self-expressive either in their daily lives or in their meditations. It is as if they were ready to explode. When they meditate in this condition, even a little flow of energy brings them discomfort. What they need to do is express themselves in conscious action, living out all their blocked images and ideas so that their energy can exhaust itself creatively and naturally. They often feel tired, too, because they are overloaded, because they have not learned how to express themselves creatively. They are too used to taking their cues from other people and thus repressing their individual energies.

We need constantly to remind ourselves that the purpose of meditation is to create a freely flowing cycle of energy. In meditation, we receive energy. Therefore, we must also transmit it by expressing it through practical actions in our daily lives. Do not hoard the energy; share it! You will then find balance and radiate energy into the world as well.

4.

Reverie

We have talked about meditation as a tool for self-discovery and observed that we should understand how to use it before beginning to work with it. This orientation will continue to be an important aspect of the discussions that follow concerning the actual techniques of creative meditation. The exercises begin with a series of methods to prepare you mentally and physically for the first part of the creative meditation cycle: reverie.

Reverie is a short, consciously guided daydream. Daydreams, like the dreams of sleep, give us a taste of the meditative experience. They feel quite real, and we can think, sense, and undergo emotional changes and reactions in response to the dream events. We have all experienced with amazement just how vibrant and convincing daydreams can be. Everyone has daydreams. In the middle of some daily activity, you suddenly find yourself in a world of your own. Usually you become aware of the daydream only after it has begun. Often you hurriedly return to normal consciousness, hoping you have not missed anything important while you were gone. At other times the daydream may be too interesting to leave, so you remain and interact with it consciously, altering it to suit yourself.

We can learn from our experiences in dreams, just as we do from any interaction. When we meditate, we heighten the dream experience by consciously setting the stage, tuning up our senses so that we are aware of everything that happens, and then becoming a willing part of the dream. The difference between reverie and meditation is similar to the difference between daydreams and sleep dreams. In meditation, we cease to alter consciously what we experience, just as we do in sleep dreams. But in reverie, we continue to direct and change the situation, as we often can in daydreams. A reverie can put us in touch with our imaginations and can concentrate our psychic energies and draw them away from distractions. More important, they help us look at ourselves objectively because we learn to assume an attitude of nonattachment during reverie.

EXERCISES

There are four basic techniques that you must become familiar with before you begin reverie and creative meditation so that you will be able to derive the most value from your experiences and encounter few distractions: the *projection screen of memory*, a means of transmuting the joys and sorrows of your daily life so that you are not concerned with them as you meditate; *relaxation*, the proper posture to assume during meditation so that bodily sensations do not interfere with your concentration; *breathing patterns*, patterns of inhalation and exhalation that are most compatible with an aware, contemplative state; and *self-analytic review*, a method for the observation and analysis of meditative experiences so that they can be applied to daily life.

1. PROJECTION SCREEN OF MEMORY

In your mind's eye, project all the day's activities, inter-actions, thoughts, and so on onto an imaginary movie screen. Most people find that they can concentrate better by closing their eyes when they experience the internal world. Begin with your first waking moment, and let your day roll by on the screen. Know that *you* are the projector. Who is the ob-server? It is also you, who are objective and uninvolved in the events shown on the screen. When you observe an event and judge it to be a negative occurrence, stop the film. Look at this frozen moment in time. Study this single image, and make an effort to see its positive side. Remember that every time a problem is born, its solution is created, too. See the solution in the problem on the screen. Perceive the wholeness of the situation by moving beyond your initial judgment of it and embracing it with an understanding of both its posi-tive and its negative aspects. Weed out the guilt you have implanted in yourself as a result of your self-condemnation. Acknowledge what you have learned from this situation and your reaction to it, and forgive yourself. Then roll the movie again, and complete the picture of the day.

What has been accomplished by this first exercise is one of the most important aspects of meditation. You have already begun to exercise a power that is one of the most sought-after rewards of meditation. You have begun to *transmute* your negative acts into positive acts. You are created anew because your understanding is expanded. Nothing we do in our lives can be washed away. If what we have done is negative, it can be transmuted to a positive thing. Similarly, a positive thing can be turned into a negative event. But whatever it is, it will always remain in the universe. Exactly for that reason, it can help us to achieve a higher level of awareness. It is so very important in this life that we bring all our actions into harmony, that we create a whole out of all the things we have done. That is why we use this technique to empty our minds every day before we go into meditation. It enables us to see what it is we have to deal with.

We must not store guilt, fear, anxiety, or resentment in ourselves. The reward for the release of these dense blocked traumas will be that tomorrow we will be acting positively on the negative acts of yesterday. The first positive profit from any negative act or event is not feeling guilt or repentance. We profit from what is negative by becoming aware of it. Repentance is more a matter of common sense than of sackcloth and ashes. First we need to be aware of our shortcomings; then, through this awareness, and with earnest effort, we can outgrow them. Repentance means that we know that through awareness we will overcome them and learn self-forgiveness. Our future is based on our experiences in the past; hence, a more positive future can only derive from a more positive view of the past.

Rather than hold onto the negative experiences of the past, you should concentrate instead on growing. Be grateful for all the results of all your actions. Guilt itself can only restrain growth. You can grow only through the interchange of positive and negative. If you use them correctly, they are equally valuable.

2. RELAXATION

Sit erect, and straighten your spine. This position is necessary to free the diaphragm so that you can breathe deeply and abdominally. Meditative states are neither sleep nor waking consciousness, so that is why you sit instead of lying down or standing up. You must maintain the direct alignment of the

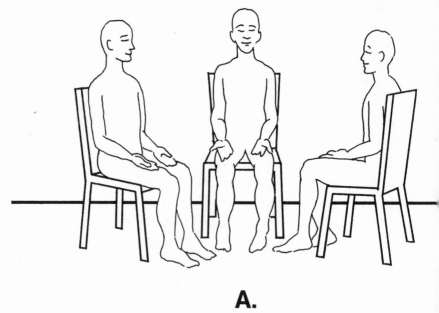

A.

Fig. 3. Posture

spine because any curve or deformation will inhibit the flow of energy through the spinal column (see Figure 3).

The goals of correct posture are to allow this free flow of energy and breath, to disperse tension, and to conserve energy. As you sit erect, support each of your limbs. If you sit in a chair, cross your feet at the ankles, or place them flat on the floor. Support your arms by resting your hands on your upper thighs, and keep your shoulders perpendicular to your spine. Remember that the spine continues into the head. Your chin should be down and parallel to the spine. This way the weight supported by the spine will be evenly distributed. Unequal distribution tends to develop pockets of tension in the body.

Even with correct posture, tension may build at the base of the spine, expressing itself in the tightening of the rectum. Deep paradoxical breathing (which will be described in the "Breathing Patterns" exercise) can be of use here because deep, slow breathing counteracts rectal tension. The down-

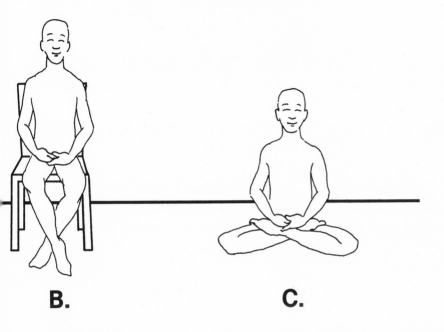

B.   **C.**

ward movement of the diaphragm will level out the rectum and prevent tension.

Our organism, as an energy-storing and energy-producing element, is much like a charged battery. Energy is discharged through extensions (wires) attached to the battery. For the human body, the extensions are the head, the arms, and the legs. In meditative states, we want not only to be relaxed but also to conserve our energy. In fact, meditation has precisely this effect on the organism: it creates additional psychic energy. Again, however, I will warn you that meditation unfulfilled by practical expression throughout the day will create an over-charge, indicated by headaches, stomachaches, and other physical discomforts.

Posture for the conservation of energy during meditation varies according to the situation. If you are meditating in a group, there need be less concern with conserving individual energy than with absorbing the energy emanating from others in the group. Therefore, the hands are resting on the thighs, palms up and open. If you are sitting in a chair, you can place your feet flat on the floor at a comfortable distance apart. When you meditate alone, conservation of energy is important, so one hand can be rested on top of the other in the lap, and the legs can be crossed at the ankles. In this way, energy is rechanneled through the organism, rather than dissipated.

The lotus position is designed to achieve these two purposes (relaxation and energy retention). If you can comfortably intertwine your legs and rest your hands inside each other atop the crossed heels of your feet, go right ahead and do it. However, I suspect that for most of us, this position is uncomfortable, sometimes even after long practice. This is a case in which responsible adaption is most obvious and appropriate. A half-lotus will do nearly as well. The goals are relaxation through comfort and (in private situations) energy circulation within the organism by keeping the body's extremities together. You cannot achieve either of these goals by forcing your body into an unfamiliar and uncomfortable pose.

When we meditate, we need to be able to stop thinking about our bodies. By achieving a relaxed flow of energy throughout our physical beings, we will not need to focus on this one aspect of being. Because they will merge into a unitary state with our other aspects (mind and spirit), our bodies will no longer disrupt our concentration.

3. BREATHING PATTERNS

Proper breathing will help to assure your spiritual development. You will have at your disposal your full intuitive and energetic capacities, and your body will be fully expressing this undiluted, unadulterated mental energy. Among the research projects in which I have participated, some concentrated on the self-regulation of physiological processes through controlled breathing. We found that the respiratory rate has a tremendous influence on states of consciousness. As the subject of these experiments, I had electrodes attached to my body to monitor changes in the electric patterns in my brain and in muscle tension and activity. We attempted to find out if certain brain wave patterns correlated with specific breathing patterns. We noted whether the breaths were long or short and when most of the air was drawn into the upper lungs (thoracic breathing) or deep into the lower lungs (abdominal breathing). The results showed that when my brain waves were in the alpha state (usually experienced as a calm, relaxed state of mind), thoracic breathing was equal to abdominal breathing, both rather slow and steady. In the theta state (subjectively experienced as a deep, still, nonattached condition with some hypnogogic images), the upper lungs were filling with air only as a side effect of the action of abdominal breathing. Oddly enough, my diaphragm was exhibiting rapid rhythmic patterns of movement at this time. When instructing my classes in different breathing techniques, I have found that altering breathing patterns is very effective in creating alterations in consciousness. This is a voluntary method of amplifying internal awareness as well as relaxing the body.

When we are not concentrating on our breathing, most of us are doing clavicular breathing. Movement is in the upper chest, in the region of the thorax where the clavicles are. This shallow type of breathing is very inadequate because it does not really fulfill our oxygen needs. The body cannot relax if it is constantly craving oxygen. In the meditative state, the energy level of the brain is not necessarily reduced, so oxygen is in as much demand as ever.

If we expand the area involved in breathing, deepen and broaden our intake using our nonexistent wings, this is *intercostal* breathing. If we use the middle portion of the rib cage, the lungs can fill themselves a bit more fully. Both shallow and intercostal breathing, however, are characteristic of the beta brain wave state. Beta waves indicate a lack of concentrated energy; there is too much tension being produced by this limited breathing to receive and disperse the amount of oxygen inhaled.

A more satisfactory pattern is *dual* breathing, which involves both the thorax and the diaphragm. By bringing the abdomen into play, we give the diaphragm more space to move downward during inhalation, allowing the lungs to fill themselves more fully. This begins to achieve our main objective, which is to make full use of all our capacities—physical, mental, and spiritual. When our lungs are thoroughly filled by each breath, even the most sensitive parts of our organism will receive prompt delivery of the energy they require in order to operate at their greatest potential.

The breathing pattern that is most suitable for meditation is *paradoxical* breathing, which is mostly abdominal and slightly thoracic. When an individual breathing in this pattern is monitored for brain waves and muscle activity in the chest and abdomen, these two indicators become synchronized. The energy patterns relayed to the monitoring machines (the electroencephalograph and the electrocardiograph) by the electrodes on the head and body are aligned, harmonized. This type of breathing may be contrary to the way you think you should go about consciously increasing your intake. It is not enough to expand your chest, to fill the lungs fully. The diaphragm has to be allowed to expand fully as well, and this can only be done by expanding the abdomen to make room for the expanded diaphragm.

To begin paradoxical breathing, inhale deeply, and voluntarily pull in your abdomen. When you exhale, push it out again. This movement is contrary to normal abdominal breathing, during which the abdomen appears to expand as the lower lungs fill with air. It takes conscious effort to reverse this normal pattern and breathe paradoxically.

Next, begin a cycle of timed breaths. The first breath is characteristic of intercostal breathing, which dominates in the alpha state, with inhalation time equal to exhalation time. Mentally count the time for each movement:

Breathe in: 1, 2, 3, 4, 5, 6, 7, 8
Hold in the breath: 1, 2, 3, 4
Exhale: 1, 2, 3, 4, 5, 6, 7, 8

As you concentrate, your inhalation will quicken, leading to this new pattern:

Inhale: 1, 2, 3, 4
Hold: 1, 2, 3, 4
Exhale: 1, 2, 3, 4, 5, 6, 7, 8

Then:

Inhale: 1, 2, 3, 4
Hold: 1, 2, 3, 4
Exhale: 1, 2, 3, 4, 5, 6, 7, 8, 9, 10, 11, 12, 13, 14, 15, 16

The ability to extend the exhalation so much longer than the inhalation shows that the inhalation must be very deep. The more oxygen you are able to hold in after a quick intake, the slower and longer your exhalation can be. The final stage of timed breathing that must be accomplished and set as a pattern for meditation is:

Inhale: 1, 2, 3, 4
Hold: 1, 2, 3, 4
Exhale: 1, 2, 3, 4, 5, 6, 7, 8, 9, 10, 11, 12, 13, 14, 15, 16,
17, 18, 19, 20, 21, 22, 23, 24, 25, 26, 27, 28, 29,
30, 31, 32

Once you have achieved this pattern and your body can exercise it comfortably, cease concentrating on it. You have regulated your breath, and it is time to move to the next stage of meditation. Even at this preparatory stage, the three-part cycle of bringing something that is unconscious to your awareness, regulating it voluntarily, and letting it go must be completed. Trust that it will retain the new form you have given it. In other words, trust yourself.

The next set of exercises will focus on another quality of breath. Visualizations that use the image of inhalation and exhalation can make you aware of the subtler psychic functions of breath as an energy that nourishes and cleanses you. Use these images (or other visualizations that you have created) whenever you feel that the particular awareness they offer you is helpful to your meditation. Alone, they are effective in producing a relaxed but energized state of being. Remember that all the exercises and methods in this book are ingredients that you can mix in your own ways for your own purposes.

While you are practicing these exercises (or any meditative technique), train yourself to disregard your breathing pattern. If you happen to notice that it is no longer in the paradoxical rhythm, do not stop your meditation in order to correct it. Complete the exercise. During the period of review, consider why a different pattern instated itself. Then, on the basis of the effectiveness of the meditation, evaluate this other pattern.

> a. Envision the air that you are inhaling to be a pale blue cloud. Inhale all that cloud. Then exhale it, carefully noticing any color changes in the cloud. Perhaps it will have turned pale gray, perhaps some other tone. This shows that you have absorbed the nutrients within it while it was in your body.

b. Expand your breathing apparatus from your nose to your entire covering, the skin. Imagine that all the pores are inhaling and exhaling. You can feel the tingling electric quality of pores popping open and closing up over every part of your body. It is very much like the sensation you experience after you have been out in the snow and suddenly come into a warm room. Feel every part of the surface of your body breathing in and breathing out the cleansing, vitalizing oxygen in the air surrounding you.

c. In your imagination, place a crystal or jewel on the center of your forehead. Now breathe through the jewel. Notice whether the inflow and outflow of air are colored. Do they undergo any changes in color? What happens to the jewel itself? Imagine it to be one color, then another, and observe what effect the breath moving in and out has upon the color of the jewel.

When you have completed any visualization or meditation, begin to come back to waking consciousness by transferring your focus from your imagination to your breathing, following it in and out, until it brings you into the external world.

4. SELF-ANALYTIC REVIEW

When you emerge into waking consciousness after any meditative exercise, begin to analyze and review your experiences in the same way you used the projection screen technique to review the day's activities. This is an aspect of the introspective feedback we gain from meditation. You might follow this series of questions:

Mental observations: What were the mental obstacles? What thoughts arose to interrupt my concentration?
Physical feedback: What were the physical obstacles?

Did I become aware of any pressure, pain, or tingling sensation at any time during the exercise? Why did this particular sensation accompany that particular aspect of the experience?

Emotional response: Did I become emotionally involved with any aspect of the experience? Did this emotion arise at the same time as, before, or after any physical sensation? Why did the feeling occur in the context of that physical sensation?

By writing down and dating these experiences, you will have a record to show you each phase of your development. Some responses, such as stomachaches, may disappear. Others, such as crying, may increase. Keep a journal to help you see your progress. If you wish, illustrate the journal with drawings of your meditative experiences.

Now that you have learned the different steps that prepare you for meditation, you can combine them into the dance of reverie. All the capabilities that have been brought to your awareness can be applied to fulfill the goal of reverie: to generate and refine a topic or symbol that can serve as the theme for a creative meditation. During a reverie, the paraconscious and subconscious minds deliver to the conscious mind images that can then be unveiled in creative meditation. In a guided visualization, unplanned changes or additions occur in the experiences of each person. These unique figures or events or objects are messages from the unconscious, spoken in a language that cannot at first be rationally understood. They need to be intensified and experienced more fully by meditating upon them.

To be an effective meditator, you must learn to accept the images, events, feelings, and perceptions that arise spontaneously during meditation. Rather than allowing your conscious mind to push them out of existence, you must work to preserve them. So be attentive—but not attached—to the unexpected aspects of your reverie experiences. These will become the most productive themes for your meditations.

Begin a reverie by assuming the proper posture for meditation. Adjust your breathing by following the sequence of patterns you have learned. It will take only a few minutes for the paradoxical pattern to be established. Then relax your vigilance over this function, and switch your focus to an imaginary point directly in front of you, about ten feet away.

Next create an environment for the reverie. Imagine a horizon and a simple scene leading up to it. Choose a landscape that is most comfortable and pleasing to you. Now imagine a path leading from you into the scene. Heighten your awareness of the scene. Notice every detail. Hear the sounds coming from the wind or the birds. Feel the warmth of the sun or the cool moisture on the grass. What time of day is it? What season? Smell the scents of the earth or the flowers or some other aspect of your scene. Create the scene wholly, and perceive it completely with every sense. If it changes, allow it to do so until it finds its own best form. This setting will become very familiar to you because it will be the setting that begins each reverie and creative meditation. If it transforms over time, allow it to do so, and acquaint yourself with it each time you meditate.

As the creator of the scene, you will remain outside it. You will guide the activities and observe what happens during the reverie. You are the director, but in this play, you are also the actor. One aspect of your role as director requires that you now create the second you, mentioned earlier. The second you walks away from you, down the path, and into the scene. Notice how this image is dressed and what features characterize it. Verify that it is you. If the image does not look exactly like you, do not change it to be what you wish it to be or think it should be. Just allow your unconscious to create the image for you.

Next check your mirror image as it walks away from you.

Call to it, mentally command it to turn around and face you as you are now, sitting in your room. Feel the distinction between the two of you and your respective roles. Now send the image into the scene again, and begin to direct the reverie.

THE MIRROR IMAGE

The creation of the mirror image is one of the most important techniques to learn for meditating creatively. I have named this method *psi-phoning*.

In siphoning gas from one tank to another, it is necessary to draw the first spurt out of the tank by force. After this initial action, gas flows without further assistance. We see this same principle at work in the psi-phoning technique. The paraconscious mind is like an endless reservoir. The individual consciousness receives its insight and energy from this source. All too often, the flow from the reservoir into our individual beings is blocked by the conscious and unconscious interference of our fears, traumas, and desires. When the energy that gives us nourishment, motivates us, and attunes us to the cosmos ceases to fill us, we suffer. We begin to stagnate like pools cut off from the running river that formed them. Discomfort, stress, and disease can result. So in meditation we try to connect the pool to the river once again. When you purposely create the connection in your imagination, it is as though you are setting out bait for the paraconscious. Like attracts like, and even an imaginary connection will be similar enough to the actual connection to create it.

In the technique of psi-phoning, we set up a conscious thought, and envision it outside ourselves. Then we energize it and activate it by directing it to change and develop. Your created image will soon begin to display details that you have not consciously conceived. This should demonstrate to you that you are now drawing information from your paraconscious connection to the cosmic reservoir. The paraconscious mind is adding new insights to the issue confronting your conscious mind.

Psi-phoning is quite literally like dialing a certain number in order to contact a more complete source of information about yourself. It is an objective action, the creation of a scenario in which you are not subjectively involved so that you can remain nonattached and thus acutely perceptive. You can continue to probe deeper for more information by consciously directing the mirror image you have created to interact with the scene in all its new aspects. Through your reverie exercises, you will become acquainted with your mirror image. You will learn that the best results are achieved when this image is the only aspect of your reverie under conscious control. Then, in creative meditation, you will be able to apply this technique to specific problems or aim it at definite goals.

Begin your practice of reverie by engaging in the visualizations outlined in the following pages, using the prefatory techniques already described to set the scene and create the mirror image. Until you are familiar enough with the examples to have your memory lead you through them, have someone read them aloud to you. That is the procedure we follow in my classes. As the students sit in a relaxed but aware condition, I describe the scene and the action to them. At first, they experience it through the minds' eye, their imaginations. Later they become so involved in the experiences they have during the reverie that they no longer need to imagine consciously; the events and their feelings and reactions to them become quite real.

When you have explored these reveries, begin to create others. Follow your curiosity and imagination, and you will produce scenarios that are especially meaningful for you.

Sculpture of Clay

Visualize your landscape, and imagine that there is a pile
of clay with water (a pool, a stream, a lake, or an ocean) near
it. Your mirror image goes to the clay and begins to mold it
into a sculpture of you. Observe the scene as the second you
mix the clay with water, knead it, and form the figure. When
the sculpture is completed, let the mirror image stand back
and observe its work. Let it make alterations, adding or removing clay, cutting, rekneading, and so on. Observe the
means by which these changes are made.

At the horizon, close to your statue, observe a bright fire.
Place the statue in the fire, and bake it. Feel the heat of the
flames. Observe the feedback you receive as you watch this.
Now the flames will die down and disappear. Feel the breezes,
and let the air cool the statue. Study the finished sculpture.
How does it differ now, after its firing, from its first form?
Note any similarities and any differences between you, your
mirror image, and this third form of yourself. When you
have thoroughly absorbed the feedback from this scene, merge
the statue into your mirror image. Then direct your mirror
image to return to you, and merge with it. Experience and
record all the feedback from this rebirth situation.

Seven Doors

Create a three-story building in your landscape. Command your mirror image to approach the building and enter
it through the double doors you will find there. Walk down
three steps, through a portal, and into a long corridor. There
are seven doors on the right side of the corridor and seven
doors on the left. All are different colors; note the color of
each. Walk down the corridor, and choose a door on the
right that you wish to open. Does the door have a label on it?

If so, note what it says. Then enter the room. Do not change anything about the room; simply observe what is being shown to you. What is there, and what kind of feedback are you getting? What does your mirror image look like? What physical sensations do you feel? What is the general atmosphere within the room? What impresses you most? What changes take place? Remember what you find in this room because later on you can always go back into it and make conscious changes. Now close the door, but do not lock it behind you when you leave.

Next choose a door on the left side of the corridor. Check to see if it has a label, and if so, remember it. Open the door, and enter the room. Investigate it. Be a good investigator; become very observant of all that you can discover within the room. After you have done this, leave the room, but leave the door unlocked so that you can reenter the room when you wish. Now walk toward the farthest end of the corridor. At this end there is a force field that, at this moment, acts as a mirror. You are confronted with a mirrored image of your second self. Observe it; take good note of all the differences among your three selves. After you have done that, realize that this is a force field you can move through. Move through it, constantly observing and recording all feedback, all experiences. Beyond the force field is a large circular room with a soft, claylike dirt floor. There is no ceiling. Walk straight to the middle of the room, and realize that you are moving from the south toward the north side. Somewhere in this room, buried a couple of inches below the soft floor, a book is hidden. As you stand in the middle of the room, become aware of the presence and location of the book. Go to it, and dig it up. Remember in which direction you moved—west, northwest, east, south, southeast, or whatever. When you have found the book, notice that it is an ancient picture book. Open it, and page through it. If any specific picture attracts you, gaze upon it for some moments, and record within your mind what it shows you. Then replace the book, and realize that you can find it again at any time.

Return to the center of the room, and walk south, back to the entrance of the room, the force field. Leave the room through this field, and turn to observe yourself in the mirror once you are in the corridor again. Again observe any changes that have taken place, and when you have done so, turn to look at the doors on the left and the right and see if everything is still as you left it. Leave the same way you came, up the three steps, out the double doors, and back into the meadow with the path. Direct the second you to return and merge with you. Once again, record all your experiences and feedback as you review and contemplate the reverie.

River and Cavern

Create a swift-flowing river in your landscape. Imagine this river to be flowing from you, bubbling right beneath you, moving toward the horizon. The banks of the river are covered with lush vegetation, and your mirror image strolls barefoot away from you along the river's edge. Feel the earth beneath your feet. Open your pores, and sense the activity of the nerve endings in your feet. You feel revitalized and energized. Far down the river, your second image encounters a cave. Settle down near the cave, and quietly contemplate it.

Eventually, someone or something will come out of the cave, awakened by your attention. Allow your second image to interact with it, and check all your reactions to it without changing, evaluating, or interpreting it. Remember what has come out of the cave. It will be an excellent theme for a creative meditation.

Notice one entrance to the cave that particularly attracts you. Move your second image through this entrance. You are in a dark passageway. Notice your environment. Feel the rough texture of the stone walls and the coolness of the air. Be aware of how you feel and what you sense. Be present in the cave. Now walk through the passageway to a cavern. There are other beings there. Experience them by interacting with them, and carefully record your actions and responses. Leave the cavern, and move through the passageway until you come to an opening into the outside world. What do you find here? Experience it, and then return to the cave, walk through the passageway and out down the riverbank. Merge with your second self.

Five Realms

Imagine that your mirror image, standing in the landscape, looks up and sees a light blue cubicle hovering in the air outlined against a deep blue sky. You float up toward it, and circle it, finding it to be the size of a small room. Note what shape it is. Discover an entrance to it, and go inside the cubicle. You float inside, as if in a vacuum. Expand your energy by imagining something that makes you feel joyous. As you float near the ceiling of the room, you realize it is water, and you move up and into this water. Soon you emerge from the water into a brilliant crystalline substance. You continue to float upward through this material as light twinkles and reflects all around you. Suddenly you have entered another substance. You move through dense gray fogs as your journey continues. Now the fog ends. You enter another level. What is its substance? How does it feel? Move through it, sharpening your awareness of it, until you enter the next realm that lies above it. Experience yourself in this realm, and observe all its characteristics. When you have finished here, slowly float downward through each of the other realms, pausing only long enough to feel them and note any changes in you or in them. Mentally record all feedback as you leave the cubicle. Merge your two selves once again.

Room of Mirrors

Again create the pale blue cubicle, and have your second self enter it. This time the interior is completely darkened. Create light within it. Illuminate it by expanding your energy, by becoming joyous. Immediately, your second self is confronted by a thousand mirrors. All the surfaces of the cubicle are mirrors. Move, and watch yourself move. Observe every detail from every angle as you are reflected in the mirrors. Record all this feedback as well as how your second self reacts and behaves in this situation. Soon, you may have difficulty distinguishing your second image from all its reflections. Maintain your objective stance as observer. Now command the true second self to exit the cubicle and return to you.

Cube and Sphere

Imagine the blue cubicle and your second self floating up to it and circling it until you are fully aware of its three-dimensionality. Your second self again enters the cubicle and expands its energy to light the interior. When it is bright enough, you find yourself in a square room, and you see that there is someone or something in it already. Do not create this occupant, but know that you resent and dislike it very much. Let your second self interact with it, and note all changes, physiological and emotional. After the changes cease to occur, notice a door in the cubicle that leads to another room within it. Enter this room. It is brightly lighted and circular. Someone or something you love very much is waiting there for you. Do not consciously choose what you find here. Interact, and collect the feedback as you did before.

Next open the door, and bring the occupant of the square room into the round room. Your second image interacts with them both. Carefully notice all that happens here, and record the feedback. Leave the cubicle, and float back to the meadow. Merge the mirror image with yourself.

PERSONAL AND UNIVERSAL SOURCES

I have found the preceding reveries to be effective for most people. But I must remind you again that you should be your own authority on how useful they are for you. Perhaps other scenarios would better evoke your unconscious. There are many ways to create reveries. One is to rely on an ancient technique for bringing people into contact with powerful symbols that reverberate deep within our consciousness: the telling of myths and folktales.

Myths tell stories, but like all ancient and traditional tales, they are told for a purpose. They transmit messages, meanings that cannot be communicated in direct speech. This is because the meaning of a myth is often a very unitive one, concerning not just the mind or feelings but a whole way of looking at the universe and therefore at ourselves. If such a tale is effective in communicating its meaning, we will resonate with some aspect of it and recognize ourselves in it. This is a roundabout way of saying that the meaning of a myth is inside you. The consciousness contained in the myth is part of that oceanic consciousness in which we are each but a drop, and every cell in our beings has a consciousness all its own. What happens to each unit of consciousness is transmitted to all the others. In this way the gods are within us.

All the various sorts of symbols—words, images, actions— have a transcendent quality. Their origin lies in a multidimensional plane that is ineffable in a three-dimensional world. But the symbolic representations of these ineffable realities permit us to intuit the transcendent reality. The symbol is a mediator. Some symbols are quite general, but you will discover the specific forms and variations that are most valuable for you.

As you begin to use myths and symbols for reveries, you will note the evolution of your experience from ordinary three-dimensional comprehension toward the ineffable stages. At first you will be able to identify yourself within the symbols and to note the specific reactions they elicit in your organism. But sooner or later you will find it difficult to express your experience accurately. You are likely to find yourself saying, "It sounded like this, or tasted like that, but that is not quite it." Yet being unable to express your experience accurately will not mean that you cannot make use of it. On the contrary, its ineffableness will indicate that you have absorbed its significance deep within you, so thoroughly and in such a diffused fashion that even you can no longer identify its perimeters. You will now know certain values and realities about yourself and the world that cannot be verified by logic or suitably rendered in words. Your intuitive capacity cannot be intellectualized and still remain vital. So to communicate ineffable experiences, you will have to resort to the same mode through which you received them: symbolic acts, words, images.

This sort of experience is obviously very personal. That is why symbols cannot be effectively borrowed by others, at least not in all their details. Each culture and each individual has to bring forth symbols and myths suitable for its particular development. We have to follow our own hearts, to take responsibility for shaping our methods of symbolic communication and making them our own. Anything less is only playacting. We must recognize our own experiences as we go through these various techniques of self-discovery, and once acknowledged, we must accept them as our own children. This acceptance will inevitably result in the development of suitable, unique techniques and symbols that will be most meaningful for each of us.

Let me briefly dispose of the notion that myths are just elaborations of dreams and that dreams, in turn, are only of psychological significance because they concern only the mind. The separation between the physician and the psychiatrist in modern medicine is just another example of the narrowing of self-understanding in our culture. For me, myths are psycho-physiological; they must affect and thus be attracted by both the body and the mind, as well as the heart. Although you may manifest yourself at one time or another primarily in a mental mode or an emotional or a physical one, you would hardly deny the fact that each time it is yourself who is acting. You are a unified energy field. If symbols are effective within us at all, they will be so at every level of our beings. Therefore I cannot agree that dreams are symptomatic of the dynamics of the psyche only; they must be symptomatic of the dynamics of the body, mind-psyche, and emotions. As a matter of fact, I would even go so far as to affirm that all diseases are caused by misunderstood myths. That is, disease is a consequence of our having lived according to a misconstrued notion of reality, of ourselves, and of our values.

What, then, is the difference between dream and myth? Both dream and myth seem to arise from the unconscious. But whereas most dreams originate in the subconscious, myths come from higher consciousness, from the paraconscious mind. Mythological potencies come from the unconscious, and they must travel through the subconscious in order to reach the conscious mind. Thus, myths are the most powerful tool for the transmission of our inner, higher wisdom to the stage at which we act according to our conscious conceptualizations. In journeying through the subconscious, myths usually attract dream qualities to themselves. The pure energy from the paraconscious mind travels through the lower consciousness, the subconscious mind, and loosens up the residue of unaccepted experiences. Then it brings those experiences to the surface so that they can be dealt with according to the more comprehensive appreciation of our world that the paraconsciously derived myths have given to us.

This is how myths activate the vital energy of the totality of our beings. Myths that have been accepted by the conscious mind are then able to express their content freely in a balanced form of emotion because emotion is the link between the mind and the body. Without emotional input, our bodies would be limited to involuntary, autonomic movement.

Let us summarize. The patterns of myths and fairy tales correspond to the consciousness of the everyday life that created them. They give symbolic expression to unconscious desires, fears, and anxieties and also to inherent potentials, such as courage and self-knowingness. Through myth, we can come to an understanding of the deep forces that have always shaped humanity's destiny, forces that will continue to determine both our public and our private lives.

It would be impossible to include in this book a well-rounded representation of world myths for you to use as reveries, but I would like to provide you with a few tales that seem to have meaning for many people. The three stories that follow are paraphrases of ancient Greek texts. As you seek other myths to use as reveries, remember that all cultures and traditions have rich sources of such tales. There are many books easily available today that paraphrase the old stories; for example, Nathaniel Hawthorne's *Tanglewood Tales,* Joseph Campbell's *Hero with a Thousand Faces,* and Rudyard Kipling's stories of India. Children's fantasy books are also often profound in their subtle symbolism; see, for example, George MacDonald's *The Golden Key,* Andrew Lang's collections of fairy tales, and all the stories by C. S. Lewis. Finally you can use the original myths in translation. The *Meta-*

morphoses of Ovid and the *Library* of Apollodorus are accessible and particularly adaptable to personal use in reverie.

Because these stories are so long and their details are so important, I suggest that they be read aloud to you or that you tape-record them so that you can listen to them when you are alone. Once again remember that your purpose in reverie is to tap the unconscious reservoir of your mind. Be attentive to all the aspects of your reverie experience, particularly to the unusual and often fleeting ones. Do not be concerned if at some point in the reading you go off into a self-created adventure and leave behind the myth and the voice reading it and all awareness of anything but your own experience. As long as you maintain your perspective as a passive spectator watching the mirror image and calmly monitoring what happens, you will reap the rewards of your meditation.

THE DRAGON AND THE SUN-GOD

Zeus, the king of the gods, loved a mortal, Leto. She bore him a glorious son and named the child Apollo. Apollo grew rapidly, as all the gods did; and when he was full-grown, Zeus sent him off in a chariot drawn by white swans to win for himself the oracle of Delphi. No place in Greece was as sacred as Delphi. From the steep slopes of Mount Parnassus, sulfurous fumes rose from a deep cleft in the mountainside. A sibyl, priestess of Delphi, sat on a tripod over the cleft, and the vapors put her into a magic sleep, a deep trance.

In her dreams, the sibyl heard the voice of mother earth coming up from the depths, and she repeated the mysterious words that she heard. Priests stood around the sibyl and explained the meaning of her muttered prophecies to the pilgrims who had come to the oracle of Delphi to learn about their future.

The oracle was guarded by the dark dragon, Python, who lay coiled around the sacred place. Old age had made him so mean and so ill-tempered that the nymph fled from her sacred spring nearby and the birds no longer dared to sing in the trees. The oracle had warned Python that Leto's son would one day destroy him. Python had tried to devour Leto when she wandered about looking for a place to give birth to her child, but she had escaped.

When the old black dragon saw radiant Apollo flying toward him in his golden chariot, he knew his last hour had come. But he sold his life dearly. He unleashed his fury, spitting fire and venom, and his black, scaly body did not stop its coiling and uncoiling until Apollo had shot him through with a thousand silver-shafted arrows. The dying dragon's venom flowed in torrents down the mountainside.

Victory was Apollo's! He had won the oracle at Delphi. Now there was light and joy on the once somber slopes of Mount Parnassus. The air was filled with sweet tunes as the birds in the sky and the nymphs of the sacred spring returned to sing Apollo's praise.

PANDORA

Pandora was modeled by Hephaestus, the god of fire, in the likeness of his wife Aphrodite, the goddess of love. He carved her out of a block of white marble and made her lips of red rubies and her eyes of sparkling sapphires. Athena breathed life into the sculpture and dressed her in elegant garments; Aphrodite decked her with jewels and fixed her red mouth in a winning smile.

Into the mind of this beautiful creature, Zeus put insatiable curiosity. Then he gave her a sealed chest and warned her never to open it. Hermes brought Pandora to earth and offered her in marriage to Epimetheus, who lived among the mortals.

Epimetheus had been warned by Prometheus never to accept a gift from Zeus, but he could not resist the beautiful woman.

Thus Pandora came to live among mortals, and men came from near and far to stand awestruck by her wondrous beauty. But Pandora was not perfectly happy, for she did not know what was in the chest that Zeus had given her. It was not long before her curiosity got the better of her, and she had to take a quick peek. The moment she opened the lid, out swarmed a hoard of miseries: greed, vanity, slander, envy, and all the evils that until then had been unknown to humanity. Horrified at what she had done, Pandora slammed the lid down just in time to prevent the last occupant from flying away, too.

The unleashed miseries descended on all mortals. Their happy, simple existence became complicated and painful as their hearts were laden with the evils that curiosity had brought them. Meanwhile, after getting over her fright, Pandora sat near the box and began to wonder once again who that last captive was. Then she heard a tiny voice from within the box. It was pleading with her, begging her to set it free. At last, Pandora could bear it no longer, for her heart was softened with compassion for the creature in the box. She raised the lid, and radiance shined out of the box. A tiny, fragile-looking being with wings as fine as beams of light flew out. The little being explained that Zeus had put her in the box with all the miseries so that if they were released into the world, she would be, too. Then mortals would have a chance of attaining happiness again. The name of the winged being is Hope.

THE BLESSING

Baucis and Philemon were a childless old couple who lived by themselves in the deep forest. One day, two travelers knocked on the door of their little hut. Although they were very poor, the couple received the weary strangers hospitably. Baucis set the table, which, because it was a very old table, had lost one of its legs; so she propped up the corner with an old crock. She served her visitors some wine squeezed from the few grape vines that grew in their yard while Philemon butchered their only goose.

This simple repast was hardly enough for four people, and soon the wine was gone. Philemon pondered how to get some more, but suddenly the wine crock filled itself up with new wine. Then the hosts realized that their guests were Zeus and Hermes. They were awestruck that the gods had come to their humble dwelling. In return for their hospitality, the gods granted them a wish.

Instead of wishing for great things, Baucis and Philemon agreed that they only wanted to remain together. Their wish was granted—and more. When they awoke the next morning and went outside, they were stunned to see that the cottage had been transformed into a palace of gleaming white marble. Overcome with thanks to the generous gods who had so blessed them, Baucis and Philemon used the palace as a temple and worshiped there until the end of their days. They died together and were transformed into two trees whose upper branches entwined to form an archway over the temple door.

5.

Creative Meditation

The preparation for meditation has now been completed. We have attended to the needs of our physical and mental selves and made adjustments in our breathing, posture, and attitudes so that meditation will be enhanced rather than disturbed. We are ready to go to work and tap the paraconscious mind, to open the channels that will let the waters of intuition enter our awareness.

As you can see in Figure 4, the stages of reverie are repeated in the earliest part of the creative meditation cycle. Although these stages have not been specifically named until now, you will recognize them, for you have already experienced them. I have purposely not named them until now so that your own experiences will have led you to the understanding of the terms. Otherwise your preconceived ideas would have limited your experience.

The reveries were developed as guided visualizations to introduce you to the inner world and help you to discover a symbol or theme from the unconscious that you could use as the topic for a creative meditation. For the following exercise, choose an image from your reverie experiences that was par-

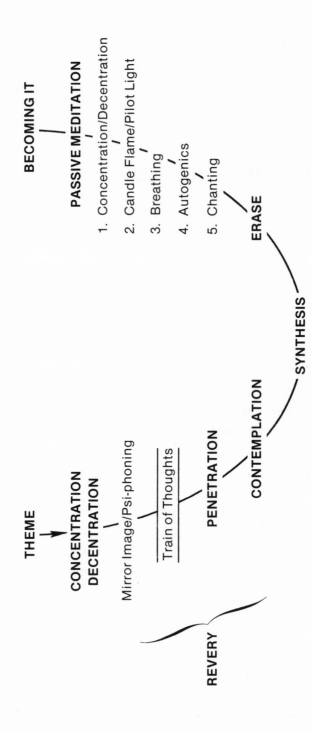

Fig. 4. Creative Meditation

ticularly attractive or mysterious to you. You could also use a problem that is confronting you or a fear that restrains you. But you will find that such a conscious image must go through a process of transformation before its true nature and source are revealed. Reverie is so essential because it can achieve that transformation. When we begin the full cycle of meditation, we can probe deeply and gain insight into the heart of the problem.

In this chapter, I will lead you through an entire meditation. Creative meditation combines the active process of reverie with a passive contemplation. Until the process becomes familiar to you, it would help to have someone read the description to you or to make a tape recording. Only one of the techniques in this final stage, the silent chanting, requires a preliminary explanation.

SILENT CHANTING

The final stages of creative meditation are designed to deepen the contemplative attitude we have thus far achieved and to ensure that neither conscious mind nor body interferes with the flow of energy and insight we can now experience. After completing the autogenic relaxation techniques of breath control and the passive volition of a particular condition of mind-body, we chant the cosmic syllable *om*.

The Upanishads tell us that the sound *om* is the synthesis of all sounds. It is the essence of all manifestations of spirit. Therefore it is known as the *seed syllable*. All potentiality and all parts of the universe are latent within this sound. If we break up the experience of *om* to understand the meaning of the syllable, we can divide it into the following parts: *om* is formed of the Sanskrit letters *a*, the subjective consciousness of the external world; *u*, consciousness of the inner world;

and *m,* consciousness of the undifferentiated unity. Actually this final awareness is no awareness because it is a condition in which the subject-object duality has ceased. There is no distinction possible; therefore there is no consciousness. This is the blissful submersion into Nirvana, or union with God, or as Buddhists say, "the state of unqualified emptiness." If we ever achieve this most marvelous condition, we will remember it as a moment of dazzling darkness. This is the void.

In spiritual traditions of all ages and places, chanting has played an important part in ceremonies and personal meditation or prayer. Sound can be used to integrate and to disintegrate, so it is a very powerful tool in the creation of different states of consciousness during meditation. In fact, the seed syllable *om* is so potent and we are so ignorant of its mysterious capabilities that I suggest to students that they chant it silently. In my classes, when I lead a creative meditation session, I chant the *om* aloud so that others can become acquainted with the tonalities and intensities that I have found most successful for me. After you have become more proficient in using meditation as a tool for providing self-knowledge, you may begin to experiment with chanting aloud. Follow the sequence of suggested types of sounds given here, but try different tones until you find those that reverberate most in your mind and body. You will recognize them immediately because they will provoke a deep, strong stillness and harmony within you. Different tones will create different conditions for you. When you learn some of the secrets of subtle sound, you will have gained an important key to the mysteries of creation.

In the process of creative meditation, *om* is chanted three times at each of four different intensities and tones (see Figure 5). These chants divide the period of silence into three episodes. Each time *om* is sounded, a deep abdominal breath is slowly exhaled in the following manner:

Inhale deeply.
Exhale as slowly as possible while sounding *om*.
Remain in the silence, breathing normally.

The different episodes are characterized as follows:

1. Chant *om* softly, at a fairly high pitch, three times. The pineal, pituitary, and thyroid energy centers are thus activated and increase the frequencies of their vibrations. This creates an intense and subtle energy that floods toward the thymus, or heart chakra, and then moves in a vortex to the base of the spine.

2. Chant *om* louder, at a lower pitch, three times. During this sequence, the emotional plane is activated. The solar plexus is stabilized, and the heart chakra begins to draw up the physical forces from the lower energy centers. Then the energy from all the centers is merged in the heart, which acts as a fulcrum to balance our mental, emotional, and physical planes.

3. Chant *om* even louder, at a deep pitch, three times. Again this sound stimulates an energy field and vibrates at a higher frequency. However this final tone affects the field that surrounds our physical bodies. This field is the double, or etheric, body. It has exactly the form and shape of our bodies and encloses us completely. The intensity and frequency of these vibrations create the aura that extends out from our bodies in many layers of color and density.

When the subtle bodies are stimulated by sound to heighten its vibratory action, it becomes a protective shield around us. We are often disrupted in our concentration by varying degrees of discomfort or subtle sensations that seem to have no source or cause. What is happening at these times is that we are receiving information through our psychic sensitivities. There is actually a physical basis for so-called psychic

Fig. 5. Chanting Om

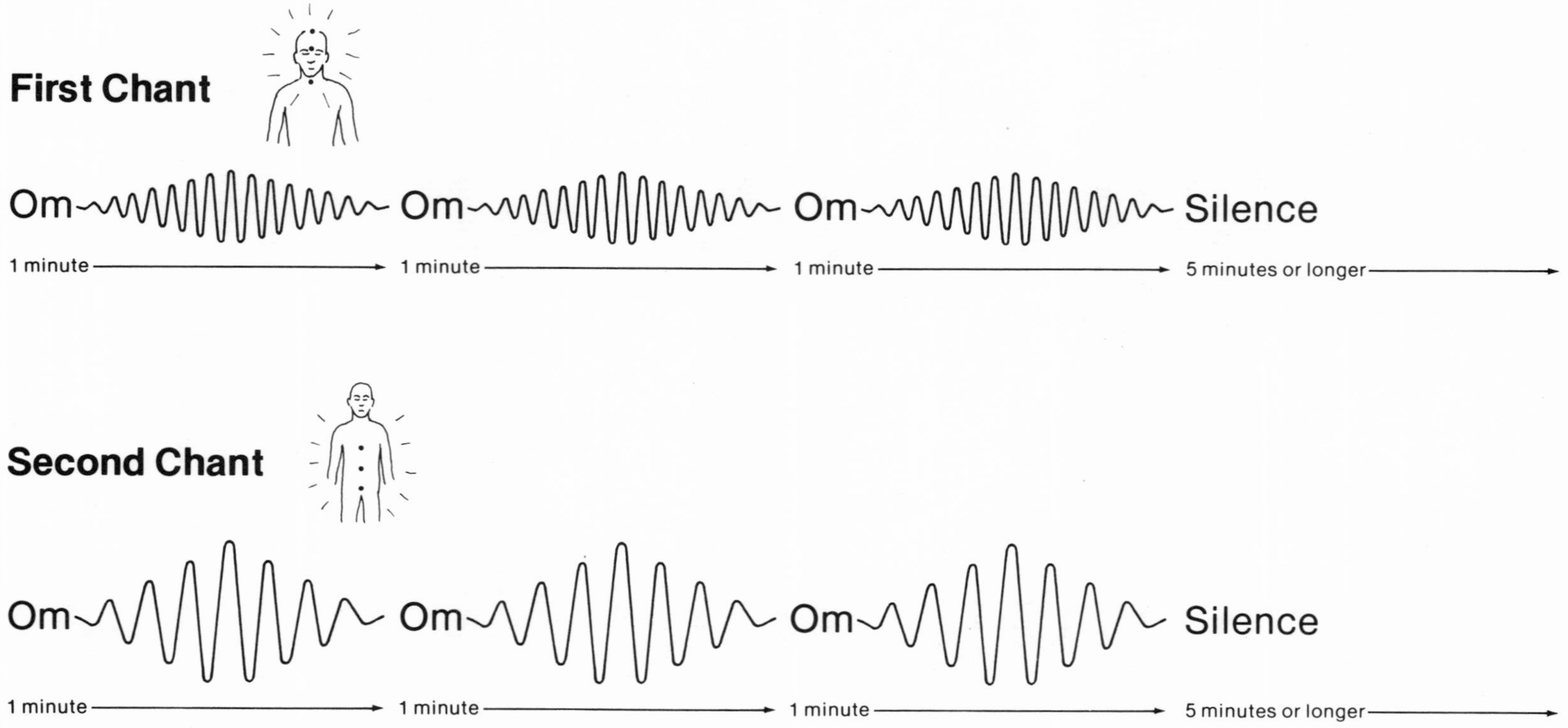

First Chant

Om～⋀⋀⋀⋀⋀⋀ Om～⋀⋀⋀⋀⋀⋀ Om～⋀⋀⋀⋀⋀⋀ Silence

|←—— 1 minute ——→|←—— 1 minute ——→|←—— 5 minutes or longer ——→|

Second Chant

Om～⋀⋀⋀⋀⋀ Om～⋀⋀⋀⋀⋀ Silence

|←—— 1 minute ——→|←—— 1 minute ——→|←—— 5 minutes or longer ——→|

Third Chant

Om ︵ Om ︵ Om ︵ Om ︵ Silence

1 minute → 1 minute → 1 minute → 5 minutes or longer →

Fourth Chant

Om ︵ Om ︵ Om ︵ Awake

1 minute → 1 minute →

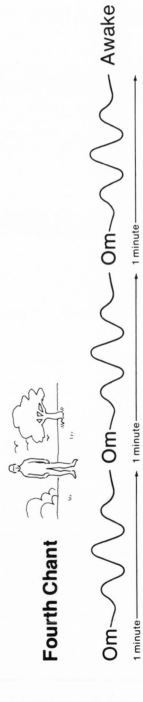

activity. The energy is as real as any other form of energy, only more subtle than our unattuned senses can notice. When we create a high, light vibration around us, no lower, denser vibration can enter our awareness. Such low energies are literally burned up; they are overwhelmed by the much greater energy field they contact.

4. Chant *om* less loudly, at the lowest pitch, three times. This final series of *om* is meant to bring you back to your waking consciousness. Meditative awareness can be so expansive, so high, that coming down can be awkward, shocking, even depressing. By sounding *om* at a very low pitch, you allow the meditative helium balloon to be slowly deflated, and your reentry is softened. You will not awaken confused and disoriented but will leave your meditation as you should. Real expansion is to have our heads in the heavens and our feet firmly on the ground.

A MODEL FOR MEDITATION

CONCENTRATION AND DECENTRATION

After the preliminaries of assuming a proper position, adjusting the breath by means of paradoxical breathing, and deriving a theme through reverie, we begin. Create a three-dimensional image of the theme, and imagine it to be a few feet in front of you. Whether the theme is a symbol (such as a geometric form) or a situation having many parts, concentrate on it so that you begin to sense its reality. Visualize every detail: color, form, texture, scent, sound, and taste. Once you have confirmed your theme, decentrate from everything else. (Decentration means not to become distracted nor fascinated by anything that may surround the object of concentration.)

Focus on the theme, and cease to be aware of anything beyond it. Avoid any logical questioning or speculation about the theme; do not evaluate it or set up expectations about the outcome of your meditation. Simply concentrate on your topic, and decentrate from any distraction (see Figure 4).

MIRROR IMAGE

As soon as you have concentrated and decentrated, create your mirror image, and see that image of yourself approach the theme. See your self walk away from you. Note how you are dressed, and make any other observations you can. Then watch as this mirror image enters the theme. At this point, and possibly at other times during meditation, a train of thoughts may intervene and impede your concentration. Handle this kind of intervention by allowing it. Do not fight it; otherwise you will spend more energy on this impediment than you are spending on your meditation. You will make it a stronger interference by feeding it energy. Allow the thoughts to flow by uninterrupted, as if you were watching a train. Calmly and passively acknowledge that there are thoughts and that as they began, so they will end. When they do cease, when the train has passed, cross the tracks, and begin again to interact with the theme through your mirror image (see Figure 6).

PENETRATION

Penetrate the theme. Direct your mirror image to merge into the scene or to contact the symbol, and watch what happens. As in reverie, remain an objective observer while your second self plays the subjective role in the situation you have created. Do not start deciding how you should behave consciously; allow things to happen, and observe how your second

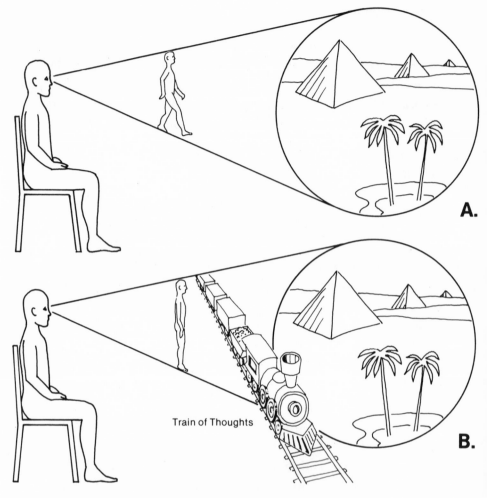

A.

Train of Thoughts

B.

Fig. 6. The Mirror Image

image is handling the situation. Unconscious changes are taking place, so just remain an observant spectator. At the same time, feel your interrelationship with what you are watching. You will get feedback within your feelings and within your own body that will further reveal messages from your subconscious mind. In creative meditation, the only psi-phoning is this initial encounter of your mirror image with the theme. Therefore do not direct the image once you have generated it.

CONTEMPLATION

Contemplate the scene before you. From your vantage point outside the action, observe, monitor, and record all that you see, hear, feel, or sense in any way. Again do not take any conscious action. Make no evaluation; cause no alteration in what you observe. Do not try to develop any details by interpreting them; if you do that, you will immediately awaken your rational, conscious mind. Your conscious mind will then charge up that train of thoughts, and it will thunder by, blocking your vision. It is also important not to censor or rule out anything that you observe. All that you can perceive is valid. It is essential that you learn to acknowledge and validate all the images and information displayed during meditation. Only then will you hear the voice of the higher mind and know that you have escaped the limitations of rationality.

Contemplation is intense, passive observation. It is actually an autogenic (self-regulating) process based on passive volition, which, in turn, is possible only through faith and trust in yourself. You do not need to verify your internal experiences by logical analysis or other people's opinions because you know that ultimately you are the only truth there is.

SYNTHESIS

After contemplating the scene and recording all the feedback you have derived from it, synthesize. Create within yourself a feeling of joyful excitement by evoking an image or event that has this effect on you. Feel joyful, feel exuberant, and then feel your energy being activated and expanding. Envision this energy radiating into the scene, at first surrounding and then permeating it with pure white light. Every detail in the scene will become clearer, and you will become more aware of the meaning and purpose of the scene as a whole.

Remember these revelations, but do not pause to consider them. Do not alter your focus of attention from the generation of the light.

ERASE

Let the white energy become so bright that it actually dissolves the scene you have been watching. As the scene is dissipated and transformed into energy itself, take a last look at it; then let it go. If anything still remains, consciously erase it. See only white emptiness before you.

CONCENTRATION AND DECENTRATION

In the midst of this white and clear space, we begin the passive stage of creative meditation. Expand your gaze, and realize that the brightness you see is actually the flame of a candle. Adjust your perspective until you see a lighted candle a few feet in front of you. Contemplate this image. Do you see how much it tells us about our own beings? Notice how the dense wax melts when the oxygen from the air combines with the energy being relased from the wick to form the flame. The subtle energy and the dense wax integrate to create the visible light. The brittle wax becomes soft, flowing, and moldable. Now regard yourself as a symbolic candle. You, too, require the energy from within your body and the oxygen from the atmosphere in order to perpetuate the flame of consciousness.

All parts of the physical world and all our sensations are indicators of a far more powerful existence, too subtle to be experienced in itself. The oxygen we breathe, for example, is symbolic of prana, the vital energy or spirit. In Eastern traditions, the word *prana* means both "spirit" and "breath." It is fascinating that in the West, a similar equation occurs. The Greek word for breath, *pneuma,* also means "spirit." Thus every breath we draw into our bodies is a symbolic expression of drawing the vital energy into our beings. When we focus on this perception of our breathing, we become aware of subtle transformations within us. Then, as in the meditation on the candle flame, we experience the merging of external and internal energies in our spines (like the candlewick), and the resulting expansion of energy fills our heads with light (like the candle flame). The higher the flame—that is, the more energy we draw from both sources and integrate harmoniously—the brighter our awareness will be. Just as the candle illumines the darkness, we radiate that degree of enlightenment that we have attained into the world. So to intensify energy means literally to expand consciousness, thereby helping our fellow beings by lighting the way.

THE CANDLE FLAME

There are many ways to use the image of candle flame to spark you into profound expansions of awareness in meditation. For example, mentally squint your eyes, and see how the light rays extend from the candle in all directions. Follow one of these rays to the periphery of your vision and then beyond. Follow it as if it were a string connecting you to its destination. What is the destination of light? It is the whole cosmos, the source and cause of the light. Follow the beam of light, and experience its source as best you can.

Similarly, you can envision the candle flame and follow one of the rays that radiate toward you, into your heart. Go with it, and feel this part of your body become warm and vibrant. Let the pulsating warmth extend into your whole body and surround you. As it does, realize that this pulsation is merging with the vibrations eternally moving in the cosmos. They are one. All distinctions between inner and outer, between you and the universe, are dissolving in this vibrating warmth.

This energy expansion also benefits us physically. The heat

from the flame melts the candle wax, and it becomes more pliable. Our own bodies will react similarly to our heat; they will become more flexible, less stressed by their former rigidity. So as you contemplate the candle flame, feel your energy unfurling into all the space around you. Feel your body gently release each tensed muscle and surrender its resistance to the warmth that is filling you.

Now consciously erase the candle. With your eyelids partially open, raise your gaze upward, as if you were trying to see the top of your head. Do not strain your muscles, but struggle to look as far up and back as you can. Most of us have become so lazy in the use of our eyes that this may be a bit painful at first. After you have practiced this exercise for a while, the muscles will be stronger and there will be no more pain. You may also begin to notice a general improvement in your vision as a result.

PILOT LIGHT

As you continue to gaze back into your head, your eyelids may flutter slightly. Do not be concerned; merely acknowledge this bodily activity as you did the train of thoughts. Focus on your purpose, which is to visualize a tiny point of light high up and back in your head. Do not hesitate to imagine the light at first. Visualize or feel this tiny spot of very concentrated energy. It is vibrating very quickly, like a tiny rotating sun or like a whirlpool or vortex. Soon it will seem as if you are looking through a long cylinder in which a spiraling groove is etched. At the far end of this cylinder is the light you first saw. Mentally direct your gaze to move down the cylinder, as if you were going through a tunnel.

When you reach the end of the tunnel, you will emerge into an all-embracing light that will penetrate into every cell of your being. You are now showered by beautiful golden-white lights. At the same time, you may observe a physiological change taking place, as energy in the form of heat begins to warm your abdomen, then your solar plexus, your chest, your neck and jaws, and your cheeks and then very slowly comes up until it feels as if your forehead is becoming warmer. Sometimes you will begin to perspire slightly, and you will notice a comfortable, relaxing warmth throughout your body. Soon this warmth will become an energy field, radiating up through your body as bright white light. It will feel as if your skull is filled with flashes of light, and you might even feel a slight expansion there.

Now imagine yourself to have a floodlight on your forehead that you can switch on. When you do, the light inside you will shine out and fill the space around you. Do not give the light any direction, but allow as much light as possible to flow from your forehead. This energy will behave like every other energy field. It will automatically form a vortex that will surround and thus expand you. Continue to acknowledge and record all your experiences passively during this time.

You are now immersed in a high, subtle energy field that no dense or lower energy can penetrate. You have surrounded yourself with a protective white light and are prepared to go within the silence.

First, we open fully by cleansing ourselves with breath.

BREATHING

1. Inhale through both nostrils, taking a deep abdominal breath.

   Hold your breath in.

   Release it with a quick sigh.

   Hold it out for a few seconds.
2. Repeat.
3. Inhale through both nostrils; hold the breath in.

ur right nostril by pressing on the right side of
nose with your finger.

e the air through your left nostril with a sigh.

it out.

ale with both nostrils; hold the breath in.

ose the left nostril.

.elease your breath through the right nostril with a sigh.
Hold your breath out.

. Repeat steps 3 and 4.

ó. Inhale with both nostrils, a deep abdominal breath.
Hold your breath in for a longer time.
Release the air with a quick, relaxed sigh.
Hold your breath out for a longer time.

7. Repeat step 6.

AUTOGENICS

Pay no more attention to your breath. Trust your body to
be self-regulatory and harmonious with the next stage. Speak
silently to yourself:

I am at peace. Yes, I am at peace.
My forehead is cool; my solar plexus is warm.
My arms and legs are heavy and warm.
Mentally I am alert, and spiritually I am awake.
Forehead cool, solar plexus warm.
Arms and legs heavy and warm.
Mentally alert and spiritually awake.
I am at peace. Yes, I am at peace.
Forehead cool, solar plexus warm.
Heartbeat calm and easy.
Arms and legs heavy and warm. It breezes me.
I am mentally alert and spiritually awake.
I am completely relaxed of soul, mind, and body,

And now I can go within.
Now I can go within the silence
And create in intervals the *om* sounds
Within my own mind and body.

CHANTING

Inhale deeply, and as you exhale, breathe out *om* slowly and silently. Focus on the sound alone; follow it wherever it goes, and feel the expansion and activation of different aspects of your being in response to it. Observe this activity, record it, and pass beyond it, always following the sound. Do not react to your physiological or psychological responses. Remember that you are here, not to evaluate or analyze, but to experience.

There is nothing to fear or protect yourself from, so do not be concerned about any strange sensations or feelings that may arise. Continue the chanting that leads to the silence. Immerse yourself in the period of silence, and reemerge to begin the next chanting sequence. You may remain in the silence for a short time or a long time. Do not worry about the length of your stay; just concentrate on allowing the energy to flow, and flow with it.

AWAKENING

When you complete the three episodes of chanting and silence, return to waking consciousness by means of a final series of very low pitched *om*s. Become aware of your body and your position. Orient yourself to your environment. When this chanting is done, gently open your eyes. Never rush out of a meditative state. Make the transition a smooth, careful one so that you remain in a balanced, clear state. If you do, you will enhance your ability to review what happened during meditation. Now is the time to recall all your insights, sensations, emotions, and visions and to notice with which aspects of the creative meditation they were connected.

BECOMING IT

Review is one part of the final stage of creative meditation. Remember what happened, and try to understand it and integrate it. This part will take a long time to complete because it goes hand in hand with a counterpart: taking action.

Creative meditation is complete only when we have acted on our insights. Each time we do, we get new feedback from the world and must review and integrate again. So creative meditation is a spiral that begins when we take conscious responsibility for our lives and set our whole aim on self-knowledge.

6.

Health and Human Energies

Creative meditation teaches us that living is the ultimate meditation. As we learn to tap the paraconscious mind as a source of creative inspiration, we will expand our awareness until we are creatively inspired in all our thoughts, actions, and words. No longer will this expansion be limited to isolated moments of focused meditation. *Every* moment will be lived as a meditation.

For most of us, this expanded awareness is still a goal, not a manifest condition. One of our greatest hindrances is our fear of change because, as I have noted, in order to grow, we must die. So in an attempt to avoid the death that is actually an essential part of living, we try to stop or freeze the flow.

The imbalances of mind and body that we all suffer at one time or another are the result of blocked energy. We close down the flow because of our fear of change or of facing reality. We begin to lose the sense of ourselves as cocreators of this world and look with dread upon the overwhelming power of a fateful, mechanical universe. We forget ourselves and become aware only of the external world, which threatens us with disease, loneliness, and failure. When we fear life, we do not grow. Finally, our rigidity can become so tense that it is expressed by our bodies in the form of migraines, heart disease, cancer, or any of the other stress-related disorders.

How can we avoid this cycle of fear and repression? We can begin by paying attention to the condition of our bodies, not just the external and obvious aspects, but the entire flow of energy that is our vital spirit. Do not focus on specific problems or symptoms. Instead, learn to become aware of where and when you blockade energy and how to release it. This is one of the most valuable applications of the technique of creative meditation.

In Chapters 6 and 7, we will demonstrate some of the ways in which active meditation methods can alleviate energy obstructions. These methods are particularly useful when they are directed toward the energy centers of the body, the chakras. If the flow through these centers is monitored and corrected when necessary, we become transmitters of energy rather than containers, batteries rather than blockades. Then life begins to be experienced as the continued process of transformation that it really is. We grow and help others to grow, too.

SELF-MONITORING

First, we need to explore some of the simplest ways to self-monitor and adjust the flow of energy. The practice of self-monitoring can begin with a procedure as simple as this: Educate your conscious mind to let you know when anything unusual is developing within your body. When you perceive a hint of malfunction, do a body check. Start with your feet, and work your way up: This foot is not moving as smoothly as the other one; my calves are too tight, and I must work on relaxing them; and so on. Mentally go through every part of your body. If you are not sure of the feedback you are getting, use a reverie. Create your mirror image, and direct it to travel through your body and check all the organs and functions. If anything seems unusual, focus on it. Surround it with light as you have learned to do in the creative meditation process, or imagine that your breath is being inhaled and exhaled through this place in your body.

If you sense a buildup of energy that could become dense and stagnant if it is retained too long, you can use another exercise for temporary relief. However, this method cannot prevent a new experience of tension if you continue to absorb dense energy without transforming it right away.

To understand why this exercise works, you have to realize that you are a human battery that can become sluggish with dense energy. To recharge this battery, you must use your grounding wires, which are your legs and feet. For these grounding wires to be effective, they should not have any insulating material around them. Your shoes should have leather soles, and your stockings should be made of a natural fiber such as cotton or wool. All plastics and vinyls are insulating materials. Therefore, if what you are wearing is insulating, you should do this exercise in your bare feet.

Your battery needs two jump wires, two energy poles, and these are your arms and hands. Although actual jumper cables are identified as positive and negative and are painted different colors, there is no material difference between them; they are distinguished only to prevent you from crossing wires. Your hands can function as jumper cables; either one can be the sending hand, emitting energy, and the other one will be the receiving hand, absorbing energy.

To begin, place one hand, open and flat, on the solar plexus, between your ribs and navel. The hand should rest loosely on this spot; there is no need to apply any pressure. This is the sending apparatus. The other hand is positioned on the back of your neck in this fashion: The inner flat pads of your fingers are placed along the cervical vertebrae, the little finger on the atlas, the index close to the first thoracic vertebra, and the other two spaced evenly between. You can think of this as having your four fingers arranged on a piano keyboard. Apply a slight pressure, and keep the fingers solidly on these points for three minutes.

During this time, your sending hand (on the solar plexus) is pushing the clogged energy upward, toward the neck. Soon a circulation develops between the two hands, loosening the energy and allowing it to be easily discharged.

After three minutes, reverse your hands and the energy flow by putting the hand that was in front on the neck and the hand on the neck in front on the solar plexus. Keep them there for another three minutes while you envision the energy moving between them.

These exercises offer short-term relief from a stagnation of energy, but if the energy flow is to be maintained consistently at optimum levels, each of the centers (chakras) must be functioning well. If any one of them is malfunctioning, the energy emission will not be pure and the energy that is being held back will stagnate, which will lead to disease. An efficient organism will diffuse outward just as much energy as it absorbs inward. Any inequality here indicates that some energy is being retained and that it is not being recycled.

All energy taken in is to be transmuted by the organism— that's *you*—and in being transformed, altered, and worked with, it is refined and then released. This energy model is a model of our lives: We have to be open to the world, to others, to ideas, activities, and energies; but just as important, we need to be expressive and involved not just physically and emotionally but also intellectually and spiritually. That small bit of circulation which you initiated by doing the tension-release exercise is a life paradigm, too: You have to be involved in a balanced circulation of your whole self with the world around you.

CHAKRAS

Using creative meditation techniques, we can make a daily chakra check and readjust any dysfunctions we discover. This can become an essential aspect of preventive medicine because it enables us to detect maladies early. But as a more general benefit, our overall energy state will become higher and more coherent. We will become more responsible, stronger, and able to assume greater tasks because we will be less constrained by incoherent moods, illnesses, and general malaise.

Each of the seven chakras has a particular way of transforming energy (see Figure 7). Starting from the top, the crown chakra (pineal body) receives and transmits energy; the brow chakra (pituitary gland) synthesizes and desynthesizes energy; the throat chakra (thyroid gland) is the expressive node for energy; the heart chakra is the area of transmutation of energy; the solar plexus chakra deals with emotional and physical energy, pain, and pleasure; the spleen chakra is the reserve center; the sacral chakra (gonads) is the reservoir. The reserve tank of energy (spleen) comes into operation only when the reservoir is empty.

The activity of the chakras results from the condition of our physical, mental, emotional, and spiritual states at any moment. Although we often hear the phrase "to open the chakras," this is not representative of what really happens. Actually no chakra is ever closed. You would not be alive if one of the chakras was closed; that would be the end of you, no matter which chakra it was. The flow of energy from chakra to

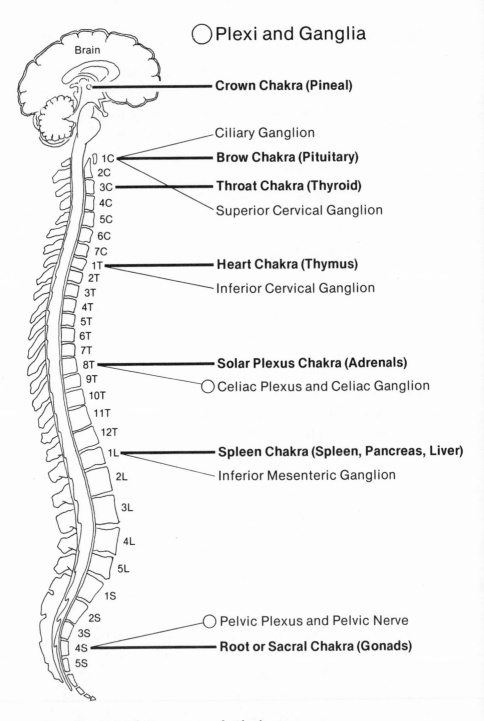

Fig. 7. Spinal Contacts of Chakras
(Endocrine Glands Related to Chakra)

chakra is continuous and dynamic. Whether it is observable or nonobservable, it exists at all times, although it might vary in its level of activity.

Extremes of overactivity or underactivity produce the imbalance that leads to disease. Underactivity represses all bodily functions because the organs are not fueled well enough to work properly. Overactivity burns up the nutrients that feed the organs. In either case the effect is the same: We do not receive the nourishment we need to continue to generate and be creative in our lives. What we seek to accomplish, then, in the meditations for the chakras, is to *regulate* the flow of energy, not necessarily to increase it.

In the chakra meditations, we identify each chakra with a color. Colors are certain vibrations of energy that are perceived by our eyes and minds as red, green, and so on. In the same way, the energy centers of the body vibrate at a certain frequency in their transmission of energy. The energy pattern around each chakra, as viewed through its aura, is in the form of a vortex. The color designated for that chakra vortex indicates the average frequency at which it operates.

The chakra vortex will very rarely be operating entirely on that frequency because the energy is being radiated in waves and rhythms. Depending on how that chakra is functioning and on its relationships with the other chakras in the organism, there will be spots of other colors at various points along the vortex. When the chakra is emitting energy in a balanced fashion, the color will be very pale, but it will be the pure color frequency that characterizes the chakra.

A pale tone indicates that the energy transmission is high, subtle, and fine. If a particular center is not diffusing all the energy that is coming into it, and if the chemistry of that center is not transforming all its energy, then the outflow will be dense and heavy. The aura of this chakra would then appear narrow and dark because the transmission is clogged and the radiation level is not very high.

The physical being is an organ for transforming energy into matter and back again into energy. The vibrations of a particular frequency that emanate from each chakra have a transforming effect on certain bodily parts. When an organ is dysfunctional, it generally means that the chakra nourishing it is also imbalanced.

The chakras are the organs of the human subtle anatomy. These power centers can be in harmonious equilibrium with one another. They produce a wave of resonance that at one level manifests itself as an individual being and at other levels blends with the entire energy fabric of our universal environment. Eastern scripture speaks of the entire universe as a giant mandala or spiraling wheel, containing myriad microcosmic wheels. The word *chakra* derives from the Sanskrit word that means "wheel." Those who are trained to perceive chakras describe them as vortices of shifting colors, sounds, and densities, rather like liquid convolvulus flowers or the surface shape of water spiraling in a whirlpool.

Each of the seven chakras has as its external counterpart one of the seven major glands of the body, whose functions interact with one another in a manner still mysterious to science. Each chakra's energy seems to be directed from a certain area in the spine (see the table below).

THE SEVEN CHAKRAS

Sanskrit name	English name	Spinal location	Organ
Muladhara	Root or sacral	Fourth sacral vertebra	Gonads
Svadhishthana	Spleen	First lumbar	Spleen, pancreas, liver
Manipura	Solar plexus	Eighth thoracic	Adrenals
Anahata	Heart	First thoracic	Thymus
Vishuddha	Throat	Third cervical	Thyroid
Ajna	Brow	First cervical	Pituitary gland
Sahasrara	Crown	None	Pineal body

We meditate on the chakras in a particular sequence. Beginning with those energy centers that are low on the body, we move toward those higher up. This physical ascendancy is symbolic of a spiritual ascendancy. The lower chakras require less conscious regulation to facilitate their activity. The higher chakras (pituitary and pineal) are certainly able to function without our conscious awareness, but they develop at a vastly increased pace when we consciously support the transformation of energy within them.

We begin with the root chakra as a way of sharpening our ability to become aware of the energy transformations taking place in our organism. As our skill grows, we will be able to shine our attention on the higher, subtler energy centers. Furthermore, there is less likelihood of dysfunction in those lower chakras, which are accustomed to unconscious, instinctive functioning. The probability of discovering imbalances increases as, through meditation, we explore the higher chakras, which require greater conscious involvement to be regulated.

The *root chakra* (also known as the sacral, base, gonadic chakra, or kundalini) is red orange in color. It is the source of the physical manifestation of life-promoting energy. Anything in nature that is red or red orange is life-promoting. It puts us into action; it generates. Because the root chakra controls the entire gonadic system, it actually activates our capability to generate life.

The next chakra, which regulates the endocrine glands, is called the *spleen chakra*. It also controls the pancreas and the liver, even though they are not classified as ductless (endocrine) glands. The spleen chakra is pink, and pink is a combination of red, the life-promoting color, and white, the all-enhancing color. So we could say that pink is composed 50 percent of the life-promoting red and 50 percent of white, the already life-promoted color, which is now expressed as radiance. Along each nerve throughout the whole nervous system, there is a kind of pinkish glow because the life energy is undergoing transmutation from the basic red orange. As it is released and becomes more radiant, it affects the part of the body that regulates the supply of oxygen, the supply of blood cells, the supply of life energy to the rest of the body.

We call the spleen the *reserve battery* because it supplements the root chakra. If the root chakra has exhausted itself or is stagnating, the spleen immediately goes into action by releasing some energy that is already in transition. When this occurs, we are given our *second breath* or *second boost*. This gives the root chakra a chance to regulate itself and then start releasing energy again. So the spleen can be as much the activator as the transmuter for energy.

The third chakra is related to the *solar plexus* and regulates the adrenal system: the adrenal glands, the cortex, and the medulla. Its color is green, the opposite of red. Green is a combination of 50 percent blue and 50 percent yellow. Blue, a cooling color, has determined but relaxing power. Yellow is another type of activating energy, related to the yellow of the sun, but it stays under control when mixed with blue. The resulting controlled energy, green, is life-preserving. Everything that is green in this world is actually preserving the life that the red has activated.

The solar plexus chakra gives exactly the right amount of energy to the adrenal gland to get the correct proportion of adrenalin in our bodies. It also restrains any excesses in the root chakra because its role is to prevent energy from being wasted. When the solar plexus chakra is overstimulated, we become too emotional, and a difficult cycle begins. The root chakra is overactivated and generates more energy than the solar plexus can handle; this stress causes a blockage that manifests as stomachaches and ulcers. In this case two energy centers are working against each other, the root generating more energy and the solar plexus holding it back. Of course, all this conflict produces disease.

The fourth energy center is the *heart chakra*. It is the color of gold, the substance humans have sought through the ages. Even the alchemist looked for gold by mixing his compounds. We could say that the gold the alchemists were looking for was expanded consciousness, the integration of "the above and the below."

The heart chakra is symbolized by the cauldron, the witch's kettle, and the Holy Grail. All that is written about the Holy Grail centers on this chakra, the place where energy is transmuted. The core energy of the lower chakras, preserved by the solar plexus, now leaps into the cauldron, where it is transmuted into the pure gold of purified energy.

The heart chakra governs the thymus and the lymphatic system, which regulate our immunological defenses. In physical and metaphysical ways, the heart is the cleanser, the integrator, the purifier. Unless the lower energies are burned in the flame of the heart, they cannot reach the higher, more aware energy centers in the body. It is here that the above and the below meet and seek union.

The first chakra beyond this point of integration is the *throat chakra*. Its color is blue, symbolizing will power and volition. Here the challenge of regulating energy effectively is related to the issue of human will versus God's will. Martin Buber called it the "I and Thou" problem. If only the Thou aspect is expressed, without the involvement of the I, we lose our individuality; we martyr ourselves in the cause of others and fail to reach our own goals. That is wrong because as long as we are on this earth, we are *of* this earth and must express our particular ego or identity. At the same time we do not want to become mere egoists.

Whatever we transmute in the heart chakra needs to be expressed. Creative expression is the domain of the throat chakra, which also governs the thyroid gland. People who do not express their creativity often suffer from a thyroid dysfunction. If they become overexpressive, without discipline or self-regulation, they will suffer from hyperthyroidism. When they fail to express themselves, they become underactive. This blocks the thyroid, and they begin to display symptoms of hypo-thyroidism, such as goiter. Because the thyroid regulates the metabolism, we can say it is the outlet for the poison as well as for the jewels within us. To be fully functional, it needs to be used for both.

The sixth center is the *brow chakra*. It is connected to the functioning of the pituitary gland, which governs the development and regulation of the fluids in the body. It also regulates the nervous system by means of the activity in the hypo-thalamus.

The pituitary is the prism that breaks down the light (energy), refracts it, and distributes it to the body through the different chakras. The brow chakra is also the synthesizer, taking the different energy components and integrating them once again.

The color associated with this chakra is indigo, which is no specific color but a mixture of the primary colors in transition. The pituitary is always busy: synthesizing, breaking down, and synthesizing again, taking a little color from this, a little color from that, a little sound from this, a little sound from that, in order to break each down and to bind it together again. The chemical aspect of the body is constantly trying to hold onto the precarious balance between hypo- and hyper-, between acid production and alkaline production. The pituitary is a facilitator in this process.

Awareness of this precarious balance, once achieved, brings great insight. Once the balance is achieved, we no longer need to expend energy in an effort to create it. We can attend to something else.

What is that something else? It is the continual (rather than fragmentary) experience of insight that in religious tra-ditions is called *enlightenment*. It is achieved by the "opening of the third eye," the full activation of the *crown chakra*. This seventh chakra is the only one with no spinal contact, and it is connected with the mysterious pineal body, which atrophies in most people by the age of thirteen because it is not used. Indeed, it cannot be used until all the other energy centers are balanced and fully functioning.

The crown chakra is symbolized by the color purple, which is a combination of red (the color of the base chakra) and blue (the color of the throat chakra, the color of expression). When the base chakra is expressed and then purified by the totality of the whole body, the result is all colors, or white. White added to the red and blue makes pale purple, the color of total integration. At the crown chakra, there is no longer a question of synthesizing, metabolizing, preserving, or promoting life. Total enlightenment results in pure white; the fire has become light.

MANDALA SYMBOLISM

To meditate on the chakras, we need to have a specific focus at first to serve as the theme for the process of creative meditation. In the chakra exercises in Chapter 7, a symbol for each energy center will be described and then developed during the course of a guided visualization that will involve you dynamically in the activity of each chakra. After you have worked with the energy of each chakra separately, the symbol-themes can be combined to form a mandala that is the focus of an integrated meditation on the chakras.

Before practicing these exercises, you should understand what your purpose is and why this particular type of meditation can fulfill it. To help you form your thoughts and properly orient yourself to your practice, I will briefly describe some of the issues that have aided me.

First, why is it effective to use the language of symbolism in meditation?

A symbol can be a visual image, or it can be expressed orally as a mantra. Like all symbols, a mantra is designed to elicit a response within you. A mantra is particularly suited for you if it can open you to a deeper area of awareness. The same general result can be achieved by all religious chants and hymns; they can awaken you, bring out some feeling, and give you new energy. It is not insignificant that the chants of the muezzin in a Muslim mosque or the Buddhist mantras or the hymns of Christianity continue to affect us. Although they might be unfamiliar to many of us, their influence is still potent. They arise from the wisdom of very old traditions, and we can still tap them as resources in our own times.

What real value does a symbol or mantra have for us?

The path of self-discovery that we have undertaken is an expedition into the unconscious mind. As with any expedition, we have to leave a lot of cumbersome things behind. We need to learn new languages and suppress our immediate derisive responses to new sights and experiences. The realm of the sub-conscious will now be our home, and this means that the habits and demands of discursive thought in the conscious mind must be temporarily laid to rest. The conscious mind is not very adept at making new discoveries. It works best as a synthesizer of data, and its tools are preconceived paradigms. To ensure that the conscious mind achieves the best results for us, we have to feed it purer data, data that we are learning to gather by developing broader modes of perception. We have to feed the mind with images of truth—in other words, with symbols.

Does a symbol contain truth? Or is it arbitrary?

The symbol is never the truth itself, but it contains truth. The symbol captures the mind and translates an unconscious message to consciousness. Notice that I did not say "one part of the mind." The symbol encompasses the *entire* mind. It acts as a means of communicating one part of yourself to another part. Each part speaks a different language, but the symbol enables them to communicate with each other. The meaning of the message is encased in a symbolic form, and the symbol will be most effective if it is attuned to those parts of the conscious and unconscious mind that need to be aware of each other. In the realm of cosmic energy, there is only one language, and symbols are about as close as we can get to that universal language.

Why is it necessary to combine the symbols into a mandala?

The use of colored composite symbols to produce certain psychophysiological effects is ancient and widespread. American Indian sand paintings have been used in healing ceremonies for millennia. The Paleolithic cave paintings in Europe are recognized as having played an important function in the caveman's ritualistic control of his world. Even today, in the traditional culture of Tibet, mandalas are primary components in the practice of medicine. A child only a few months old will be taken by his parents to a lama, who looks at the child's energies and potentialities by various shamanistic means and ascertains what the child has in excess and what he or she lacks. He then creates an appropriate mandala. For example, perhaps he sees a tremendous amount of royal blue in this child. He realizes that the child is going to be difficult to manage because he is very willful, and his excessive willfulness may not be sufficiently restrained by intelligence. Therefore the lama incorporates a color in the mandala that counteracts this willful blue. Or perhaps there is a lack of creativity. The lama then applies another appropriate color or symbol, one that will stimulate creativity. The completed mandala is shown to the child and hung above his or her crib so that it will be the first thing he or she sees when waking in the morning and the last at night. Later on the same mandala will be the subject of the child's first meditations.

The chakra meditations, then, are based on venerable traditions. Meditators today are not the first to meditate upon specific symbols in order to heal themselves or attain a greater understanding of the universe and their roles in it. I often suggest to my students that they follow this Tibetan example and make their own mandalas and to position them in their homes where they can see them comfortably and frequently. If you create your own mandala after experiencing the chakra meditations, use it as an object for contemplation, but remember that it will affect you every time you glance at it. Because your mandala can have this potent influence on you, it is important that you construct it carefully from the insights you have gained in meditation.

How can we use the chakra checks to perceive and regulate the internal status of our minds and bodies?

Each visualization begins with a breathing exercise. We breathe into the theme-symbol and fill it with vitality and the color associated with that chakra. Next we dissolve the color into whiteness. If a particular chakra resists the whiteness (which is the representation of the pure energy of our total beings), this indicates a blockage. You should not go on to the next chakra until you have analyzed this chakra more thoroughly. It is possible to discover the nature of the resistance and then to banish it. Only your own meditative experiences can be your teacher in these tasks. You should be able to experience direct feedback from each chakra as you focus on it. This feedback will be physiological as well as psychological and will teach you how to detect any imbalance in the chakra.

To the extent that each chakra is functioning well, you will experience an increase of energy. As I have explained, the energy peculiar to each chakra expresses itself along the spectrum of a specific color, which grows paler (whiter) as the level of energy increases. Of course at first you may not be able to explain what the feedback means or even where it is coming from; but if you continue with the method, you will see an overall improvement in your body's conditioning. As energy is refined, the level of our consciousness expands, and we are ready to attend to the higher vibrations of the upper energy centers. This is the reason we meditate on the chakras in sequence.

The chakra exercises in Chapter 7 are designed to help you learn to regulate yourself. We benefit from the acquisition of these regulatory skills because we can create more harmony between all the aspects of our minds and bodies. Self-regulation is not self-control. We do not want our bodies to control our minds or our minds to control our bodies. Rather, we want each aspect of ourselves to speak freely. Then our total energies will be available for voluntary disposition.

7.

Activating the Chakras

As you begin to practice the chakra meditations, remember your purpose in meditating. If you have carefully followed the instructions for creative meditation, you are ready to implement it in the potent visualizations that follow.

You can approach these visualizations in more than one way. Until you become fully familiar with the sequence of events in each exercise, it might be beneficial to have someone read the exercises aloud to you. Some people find that they have intense experiences when the exercises are read aloud. However this method has a drawback. You may find that certain aspects of the visualization require more time than others; if someone else is guiding the exercise, you are not completely free to explore the directions that your internal experiences are taking. Another approach is to read the instructions before you meditate and become thoroughly familiar with the sequence of images. Then, when you meditate, the exercise almost seems to direct itself. One way to improve your memory of images is to make models of them; draw, paint, or sculpt the figures that are used in the exercises. The composite mandala of these images, which is shown on the back cover of this book, displays the correct colors associated with each chakra. Use this figure as your guide, and create your own images of these symbols.

ROOT CHAKRA (GONADS)

THE SYMBOL

Root

For this meditation, the symbol is a square that we extend into three dimensions. So imagine that the square is becoming a conduit, like an infinitely long ventilation shaft. Envision this shaft as beginning right in front of your face. It is the same size as your face. Imagine that you are in a room without oxygen, so that you have to put your face close to this ventilation conduit to breathe.

This image of the three-dimensional square may not be stable on the screen of your mind. As soon as you imagine it, it may change into something else. Do not try to force it back into the square shape.

Over the years that I have given these exercises, I have found the square to be a persisting image for this chakra. But in some people, the imagination may transform the square into another shape, one more appropriate for other energy levels and other chakras. As we discovered in doing the guided reveries, there is no sense in controlling these images; in fact, it is their spontaneous modifications that create the feedback we need in order to learn about ourselves. So if you lose the square image, do not worry about it. Let it be whatever it will be.

The oxygen flowing from this square conduit will have to be a particular color: red orange. How this color presents itself inside the conduit is not important; you can imagine it as a liquid, a gaseous, cloudy substance, or just a colored light. Because you are going to be breathing in this substance mentally, it will probably be gaseous in form; but again, do not inhibit its transformations.

BREATHING

When you have created this image and its coloring, take three deep breaths (three inhalations and three exhalations). Keep your mouth open, and breathe through it. The nose will also be breathing, but do not concentrate on what your nose is doing. The reason for using the mouth is that we get more physiological feedback this way; we may even experience a sucking or drinking sensation. Breathe through your mouth in all seven of these meditations. (This is not normal for other meditations, but the purpose of these specific meditations is to connect your awareness to your internal energy patterns through the imagination. If we are going to learn to trust our imaginations, we need a great deal of physiological feedback to show us that they are working.)

Ideally, you will be doing paradoxical breathing in all these exercises. If you are not yet comfortable with that pattern of breathing, then breathe normally. The most important thing is that you focus all your attention on your internal feedback and rely on breathing that has become instinctive and unconscious.

THE MEDITATION

1. Sit in a comfortable position, spine erect, head held straight. Close your eyes, and create the image of the square, an infinitely long conduit, a few inches in front of your face. Now fill that conduit with the red-orange substance.

2. Breathing through your mouth, take in a deep abdominal breath. Suck all the red-orange substance out of the square, and take it down all the way to the base of the spine. Let it settle in, and hold it there. To enhance your imaginative control over this air, imagine that the entrance to the root chakra, the base of the spine, has a door that opens up when you breathe in and closes when you have stopped, trapping the air at the bottom of your body. This way, it will not escape until you are ready to exhale.

3. Exhale deeply into the square conduit in front of your face. Wait a moment before inhaling again. During this time, observe what has become of the exhaled oxygen as it floats around inside the conduit. Has it changed its color at all? Or its form? Or its quantity?

4. Second inhalation: Repeat the first cycle, breathing in the colored substance from the square (however much of it there is), letting it go down to the base of the spine, and holding it in. Now gaze back into the square, and blow the substance out of your body and into the square. Take note of any psychological and physiological changes. These will be revealed by any changes in the form of the conduit, the nature of the substance, or the color of your breath.

5. Third inhalation: Repeat as before. This time, however, when you exhale, blow the substance around the sides of the square conduit. Keep your attention on the square while your breathing returns gently to its normal pattern. Carefully observe any changes taking place in the image.

6. Mentally take note of the rest of your body, inside and out. Any areas of your organism that are emitting an unusual amount of sensation will come to your attention. Note what those areas and feelings are. At the end of this exercise, you may feel more energetic and notice a rise in temperature. The heat you feel will probably be in the lower abdomen or the buttocks.

FEEDBACK

If the substance being breathed changes from red orange to any other color, you can identify the origin of the new color from the other chakra exercises. The chakra that is symbolized by that new color has been influenced by your excitation of the root chakra. If blue, the color emanating from the throat chakra, enters your image, it may indicate that the throat chakra is not allowed to express itself properly. Consequently its energy seeps out into other areas of the organism.

If a dense, deep tone (such as purple or brown) intervenes in the red orange and there is no white in the final exhalation, it indicates that there is an energy block in another chakra. If the red orange does not become pale or even white, it means that the root chakra is blocked. It is absorbing energy adequately but not radiating it. Remember that although deep tones may be pretty, in this realm they indicate dense energy or sluggishness. Health is always indicated by brightness, fast energy, and intense radiation, all merging into white.

By the third exhalation, all color may have disappeared. Instead, you might see black or white or a gray substance. When the final exhaled breath colors the square white inside and outside or white on the outside and black or gray on the inside, you have attained a balanced condition in the chakra. However if the last breath appears white inside the square and black outside, you are not emitting any energy into the environment, just absorbing it. This image indicates that you are holding in energy.

These exercises are designed to be performed in sequence, and there is no reason to stop at any one chakra. So when you set out to do these exercises, take enough time to complete the cycle. If you do not achieve whiteness at the end of any single chakra exercise, then that chakra is imbalanced: you should not go on to the rest of the exercises until you exhale white at the end of each one. If you do go on, the feedback on the other chakras will be imprecise because of the dysfunctioning of the imbalanced chakra. So sometimes the cycle will take longer than you expect.

SPLEEN CHAKRA

THE SYMBOL

Spleen

The next symbol is the triangle. For the exercise, imagine a transparent or translucent pyramid with four sides and a bottom. This pyramid will have to be big enough for you to sit inside (in whatever position you choose). You may prefer to create a second image of yourself and observe this figure sitting inside the pyramid. Most people have a more intense experience, however, if they imagine themselves inside it.

When the image is complete and you are sitting inside, fill the pyramid with a pink substance, either all at once or gradually. You might imagine this process as being like water rising from the bottom and slowly covering you.

BREATHING

Begin breathing as in the first exercise, taking in all the pink substance through your mouth and letting it fill your insides down to the base of your spine. Then let the pink substance lift up a bit, up to your hipbones and your waist. During the root chakra exercise we imagined that there was a door holding all the red-orange substance in. Just above that trap door for the gonads, there is another door for the spleen. The flexible tube that is bringing in the pink substance reaches to the base of the spine. After the substance flows all the way to the bottom of the tube, it flows back to the level of the spleen door, which opens to receive all the pink and then shuts tightly to hold onto it for a little while.

In all the exercises after the first, you inhale or pull down the colored substance to the spinal base and then let it rise up to the appropriate chakra level (hips for the spleen, solar plexus for the heart, and so on). Quite often by the time you have packed in all your energy at the spine, you have finished inhaling and cannot breathe in more while you are raising the substance to the higher level. If that occurs, just hold your breath while the substance is rising from the spinal base to the chakra level. (In the first exercise this was not a factor because the spinal base itself was the chakra level.)

When you exhale the first two times, blow the pink out all around you, but do not blow it up to the top of the pyramid. Just concentrate on filling up the pyramid beginning with its four corners. On the third exhalation, blow the pink upward, up and out of the pyramid.

THE MEDITATION

1. Before you begin this meditation or any exercise involving the imagination, quickly check your body to detect any tension points, pressure spots, itches, or other physical discomforts. If any part is not relaxed, try to relax it. This is very important. In order to become self-regulatory, you have to learn to detect what the body is telling you.

2. Sit properly, with your eyes closed, and imagine yourself sitting inside a clear pyramid. Then fill it up with a pink substance.

3. Taking a deep abdominal breath through your mouth, inhale all the pink substance, and let it go down to the base

of the spine and then flow back up to the hips. Before you exhale, make a mental check of your body and your imagined
surroundings to detect any changes in feelings or perceptions.
Is your body changing at all as it sits inside the pyramid? If
there is any development, mark it so that you can observe it
again during the next two breaths.

4. Now exhale, and blow the pink all around you, into
each corner of the pyramid, but do *not* blow upward.

5. Inhale and exhale a second time, just as before.

6. Now inhale deeply for the third time, and while the
pink is flowing to the base of your spine, observe what is
happening in the pyramid, on the outside of your body, and
so on. Then exhale, this time up and out of the pyramid. As
your breathing returns to normal, quietly observe what is
happening inside the pyramid and to you.

FEEDBACK

During inhalation in this exercise, you will most likely feel
a constriction around your body, as if you were being fitted
into a tight glove. When this happens, there will be a notice-
able denseness and darkness around the body and a corresponding brightness inside the pyramid, emanating from the corners.
This indicates that you are drawing all the pink energy into
yourself, creating a cloudiness around yourself and making
the pyramid hazy, either white or gold.

When you exhale, you will become subtle and light again,
having unloaded all this energy back into the pyramid. This
experience is rather like being underwater and holding yourself down, then letting go and rising to the surface, buoyed up
by the water. Another common experience is a tingling sensation all over the body.

Those who have the capacity to observe the human body
and see through its external shell, so that it is as transparent

as the image of the pyramid, state that they see a pinkish glow over the entire body.

After the final exhalation you should eventually observe only white, but the pyramid shape will be less distinct than the square was. In an extreme experience, the pyramid will hardly be visible at all after the third exhalation. There will be white everywhere, inside and out.

The reason for using the pyramid shape is that it is roughly the shape of a person sitting in the lotus position. Thus, when you blow that pink substance out the top of the pyramid, you are blowing it out the top of your own head. The significance of this will become clearer when you experience the exercises on the higher located chakras.

SOLAR PLEXUS CHAKRA

THE SYMBOL

The image for the solar plexus is the circle. For the exercise we work with a green cylinder. Begin by imagining that you are standing on a small, green, circular field. Surrounding you, at the perimeter of the field, is a green coil that looks

Solar Plexus like a vertically stacked Slinky a few inches high.

BREATHING

During your first two inhalations, imagine that you are bending down and lifting up the green coil, raising it to form a green sleeve around you. After your breath has extended the coil so that it envelops your entire body, fold the upper edge over so that it forms an inner sleeve closer to your body as you draw it down to the level of the base of your spine.

Then bring it back to the level of the solar plexus, and hold this position for a moment. When you exhale, let the inner sleeve retract to the fold, and then let the coil slip down to rest at your feet again.

On the third inhalation, give the green coil a twirl as you lift it so that it spins in one direction very quickly, either clockwise or counterclockwise. It will rise to the top of your head and curl over, stopping at your hips and then rising to the solar plexus. It will be like a vast green Hula-Hoop twirling around your midsection. When you exhale, push the green hoop upward, but instead of pushing it over your head and down, let it go twirling off above you.

This may seem to be a difficult image, but there is a reason for its form. Originally I instructed people to breathe in the green cylinder as in the earlier exercises. But this pattern tended to trigger an overemotional reaction; people became very excited and lost their concentration. Consequently I have altered the exercise so that it takes place entirely outside the body, which remains a solid axis with the cylinder rising and falling around it. Even this way, I notice some people responding with tears, which is quite all right.

THE MEDITATION

1. As always, relax your body, and mentally check it all over to see whether there are any tension or pressure spots. Relax them.

2. Sit in a comfortable position, close your eyes, and begin paradoxical breathing. Take a few deep paradoxical breaths to ensure full relaxation.

3. Now envision yourself standing in a small, round, green field. If this proves difficult, imagine a second image of yourself standing in the field. Stacked up around your feet is a

green coil. Inhale deeply through your mouth, and as you do, bend down (in your imagination), grasp the top of the green coil, and raise it over your head. Then fold it over, and let it fall close to you, down to your solar plexus. Still holding your breath, lift the coil up a bit, beyond your waist, and finally up to the solar plexus.

4. Be sure to notice what is happening around you while you are holding your breath. Is the color of the coil changing at all? What about its shape? Do you feel any sensations anywhere on or in your body?

5. Exhale, blowing the coil up over your head; then let it fall to your feet in a stack, just as you first found it. Observe and note any changes or feelings, especially psychological reactions.

6. Inhale and exhale again, as before.

7. The third time, as you inhale and bend down to grasp the coil, set it revolving quickly around you. While the coil is twirling, lift it up with your hands and your breath, up over your head and down inside itself, to your spine, then up to the solar plexus. Hold it there, and observe. Exhale, blowing the green coil upward and letting it twirl out of sight. As your breathing returns to normal, quietly observe everything that you can see or feel.

FEEDBACK

Among the possible color changes that will occur in this exercise, the intervention of yellow or gold is the most common. This indicates the presence of energy from the heart chakra, which is easily activated when we concentrate on the solar plexus.

Because of the complexity of this particular exercise, many people have trouble exhaling all the green energy. If any remains, there will be some pressure or pain in the chest, neck, or forehead. If that occurs, make a greater effort each time you do the exercise to blow out all the energy you have taken in and to note any blockages as the energy flows upward at the end.

HEART CHAKRA

THE SYMBOL

Heart

The symbol for this chakra exercise is the cross, and the color is golden yellow. In Western religious traditions, the cross usually has a short horizontal bar and a long vertical bar, symbolizing an energy pattern that runs mostly up and down, with little expansion sideways. But, the cross for this exercise has four equal arms, emphasizing the full extension of our energy discharges, both upward and outward. To put the heart energy into a state of equilibrium, symbolized by this cross, requires not only an awareness of incoming energy (the vertical bar of the cross) but adequate expression of that awareness to the world around you (the horizontal bar).

(I might add that the symbols for this series of chakra exercises are building a mandala: the square on the bottom, the triangle over it, the circle over the triangle, and now the cross over the circle. These last two form an orb, a symbol of justice, wisdom, and universal peace.)

For the heart chakra exercise, imagine the cross with its four equal arms. Three of them, the top and the two side arms, are open at the end. Only the bottom end is closed. The cross should be as big as you are or bigger and very close to you. You may want to imagine it as a hollow, transparent cross so that it can be filled up. Extending from the center, or just below the crossbar, is a tube or straw.

Now fill your cross with a golden-yellow substance (liquid, gas, or light).

BREATHING

For your first two breaths, suck hard on the tube, and inhale all the yellow substance, packing it down to the base of your spine. Then, while holding the breath, allow the yellow to rise to the level of your heart and settle there. Observe any changes, and exhale back into the cross. For the third breath, inhale as before; but when you exhale, blow the yellow substance out so powerfully that it spurts out all three open ends. The yellow substance should spurt out so forcefully that it creates a flame, transforming the cross into a fleur-de-lis of energy.

In all the exercises thus far, the final breath has had extra work to do: The red-orange substance had to be blown around the edges of the square instead of into it; the pink had to be blown out of the top of the pyramid instead of filling it up again; the green cylinder had to be sent twirling into the air instead of placed back down on the ground. In this exercise the yellow must be sent spurting out through the three open ends of the cross. Obviously, then, the final exhalation is faster and more powerful than the first two in every case. You are not merely exhaling; you are blasting your breath into the symbol and beyond.

THE MEDITATION

1. As usual, prepare yourself by sitting comfortably, closing your eyes and beginning paradoxical breathing. As you begin these practice breaths, exhale with an audible sigh, and let your whole body become limp and relaxed. Check your

body, and relax any tense points. Exhale fully, and pause a moment before beginning inhalation.

2. Imagine a large cross, with four equal extensions. Fill it with a substance that is the golden-yellow color of honey.

3. Open your mouth, and sucking on the tube at the center of the cross, inhale deeply, making sure the yellow substance goes all the way down to the base of your spine.

4. As you hold your breath, allow the substance to rise to breast level and settle around the heart. Observe any changes in the color or quantity of the substance or the shape of the cross and any physical and psychological reactions in yourself.

5. Slowly exhale, pushing the yellow through the tube and back into the cross. Continue to observe the process, noting any alterations or reactions.

6. Breathe in again, and repeat the cycle.

7. The third time, inhale briskly, as before. Pause a moment before exhaling; then blow the yellow forcefully through the tube so that all of it spurts out of the cross, spraying from each of the three open sides.

8. Let your breathing return to normal as you continue to observe yourself and the situation.

FEEDBACK

The heart chakra is the fulcrum of the transmutation of energy that occurs constantly in the body. Thus, when we begin to excite this center, many physiological changes may be stimulated. For instance, you may perspire a bit more during this exercise, especially through the hands or chest. This is a way for the body to exude toxins. You may also feel a very acute blockage of energy flow at the neck, more than during the previous exercises. As a result, you may have some pain or tension there by the time you are done. The next chakra, the throat chakra, is the expressive one, and has not been sufficiently stimulated; so released energy gets stuck there.

Of course color is the most important thing to observe. Did any colors other than yellow intervene? Did the golden yellow change to white, silver, or gray? At the third exhalation, the substance spraying out may take the form of bubbles, an effervescence of silver bubbles. This indicates that energy has been purified, and the result will be a feeling of intense well-being and peace. The impurities in your system may be loosened by this time, and this lump of impurities may give you quite an internal jolt when it is released. Then it will be broken down and released as a burp. You may have a dizzy feeling, too; but this will happen in any of these exercises if the center involved is being awakened from a previously sluggish state.

THROAT CHAKRA (THYROID)

THE SYMBOL

Throat

The symbol for the throat chakra is a crescent, and the color is blue, the color of volition. The throat is the expressive center. At this final stage of transformation, our energy is made ready for expression. The thyroid is very important because it governs not only the body's metabolism but also the metabolism of consciousness. What the organism expresses through the thyroid is all the energy that has been pulled up by the heart from the lower energy centers (gonads, spleen, solar plexus). In order to maintain a balance of energy in the organism, what has been absorbed from the environment must be returned to it.

A person whose thyroid chakra is out of balance with the other chakras would be very destructive not only against society but also against himself, owing to his unbridled will-power. The organism's energy must be mellowed and directed by the two higher energy centers, the pituitary and pineal chakras. However the strength for expressing the energy comes from the lower chakras. The heart chakra is the transition point where the purification process begins.

In the mandala evolving from our chakra symbols, the crescent represents the cup of a chalice known as the Holy Grail. It contains the wisdom necessary for us to evolve from unconsciousness to full consciousness. The base of the pyramid forms the base of the cup, and the cross is the stem of the chalice that supports the bowl.

For this exercise, the crescent takes the three-dimensional form of a cup; it will be filled with a dark blue substance (you will probably want to imagine this as a liquid).

BREATHING

During each inhalation, you will imagine yourself picking up a very large chalice, tipping it to your mouth, and slowly swallowing all the blue liquid. These inhalations will have to be cautiously spaced because they should be slower than those for the previous exercises. This blue liquid is very precious, like rare wine, and you want to savor its taste fully, without rushing. Not a drop is to be spilled.

In your imagination, let the blue liquid descend all the way to the base of the spine. Let it rise; it will be exiting thyroid. Pause after the long inhalation, hold the liquid in, and then exhale, letting the liquid rise back up through your throat, over the thyroid, and back into the cup. Follow the same pattern for the second breath.

On the third breath, you will try to retain the liquid instead of letting it flow back into the chalice. You have become a glutton, so you gulp down the liquid and let it rest inside; then, as it starts to come back out, you gag once, making it pause in your throat before you let it run out of your mouth. As you let the liquid go, the cup also passes away.

To gag, merely activate the glottis momentarily, as if you were gulping, and exert upon it the pressure of your breath trying to escape. When you have gulped or gagged once, the release will bring a rush of air, *ahhhh*. At this point the imaginary liquid will flow out. Because we are internalizing this entire process anyway, there is no need for any noisy sound effects in this third exhalation. The only sound you might hear yourself making is that slight *ahhhh* as you release the glottal constriction and exhale.

THE MEDITATION

1. Sit comfortably, shut your eyes, and imagine a large chalice in front of you. It is large, but you can still lift it by using both hands. Now fill the chalice with a deep, royal blue liquid. The color may start to change right away. Do not make any effort to control it; just observe and remember.

2. Inhale slowly and deeply, drinking the cool blue liquid that passes over your tongue and descends far down inside until it settles at the base of your spine. Savor every swallow, and hold it in; pause to observe any reactions in your body. Then exhale, letting the liquid rise and flow back into the cup without making any effort to push it. Pause again, and watch the texture and color of both the residue of the substance and the cup and of course your own reactions to the process.

3. Inhale and exhale a second time, just as before.

4. For the third breath, you become very thirsty and take in the last bit of the liquid with a strong inhalation, gulping it down all the way to the base of the spine. Pause; then as you begin to exhale and the liquid rises, lock your throat at the glottis, as if you were beginning to swallow, but retain the

substance. Then relax your throat, and let the liquid flow out under its own force. Now relax your breathing, but continue to observe the images in your mind, as well as your physical and emotional reactions.

FEEDBACK

The blue liquid may turn into many other colors, depending on the extent to which the other chakras may be stimulated or connected with the activity of the thyroid gland. As we saw with the solar plexus, the stimulation of a particular chakra may have an effect on the chakra directly above it. The dark blue of the thyroid may turn into a very dark purple or brown, which usually indicates pituitary gland interaction. As we will see later, the color associated with that chakra is indigo, a color in transition between purple black and brown purple. When this color affects royal blue, the result may look black or murky, but you should try carefully to detect what color tones are hidden in the blackness. A healthy condition of the throat chakra will be indicated by a pale blue in the exhalations.

Do not be concerned if more liquid flows back into the chalice during exhalation than was originally there. This is a common experience.

BROW CHAKRA (PITUITARY GLAND)

THE SYMBOL

Brow

The symbol for the sixth energy center, the brow or pituitary chakra, is a six-pointed star, and the color is indigo. This is the Star of David, of course, or the Star of Creation. In Cabalistic symbolism, the inverted triangle represents an empty receptacle, and the other triangle represents energy radiating into the receptacle and filling it.

Energy enters the organism at the top and travels downward, disintegrating as it goes into the seven subtle forces, which correspond to the seven chakras. Once it has reached the lowest point, we are responsible for synthesizing this energy and expressing it, following the same route the energy traveled as it entered and diffused itself within us: from the gonads, spleen, and solar plexus back to the heart, the throat, and now the pituitary gland, which accomplishes the final synthesis before expression through the pineal, or crown, chakra. Thus the six-pointed star is a suitable symbol for stimulating the brow chakra because the two triangles represent incoming and outgoing energy.

For this exercise, however, we will concentrate on the star image as a whole. Imagine this six-pointed star as being the floor plan for a tall, roofless room with twelve walls corresponding to the twelve sides created by the six points. If it is easier, think of the star as a giant cookie cutter that is a foot or so higher than you are. You will imagine that you are sitting in the middle of this tall room, and each of the six corners will be filled with the indigo substance.

BREATHING

As you begin breathing deeply, with your eyes closed, you will start to turn. If you need to, you may picture yourself sitting on a revolving disc. Turn just fast enough to make one full revolution with each inhalation, and as you turn, suck in the indigo from all six corners in one breath. Let the indigo settle at the base of your spine. Then, holding your breath, stop revolving, and let the indigo rise all the way up to your brow. Concentrate on your interior feelings. As you exhale, start turning in the reverse direction, and blow the substance back into the six corners as you revolve past them. If your exhalation is much slower and longer than your inhalation, you can complete two revolutions while exhaling.

It does not matter in which direction you start turning when you inhale. Follow your natural inclination, which will depend on which hemisphere of your brain is dominant. Once you have started the exercise, do not interfere if the color of the substance turns from indigo to something else or if you start turning in another direction. Just observe all these alterations so that you can review them later.

On the third breath, continue the pattern of taking in your breath more briskly and blowing the substance out forcefully; but blow it up and over the top of the walls, not back into the star-shaped room. This room has no roof; hence the substance can float right up when you finally release it.

THE MEDITATION

1. Sit comfortably, and practice deep breathing, inhaling paradoxically. Release your breath with a sigh. Repeat.

2. Shut your eyes, and imagine yourself sitting inside a six-pointed star. Build up its walls until they are higher than you, but do not put a roof on the top of this room. Fill the room with an indigo-colored substance (liquid, light, or gas). If you have trouble imagining indigo, start with red and then add blue to form purple; then add green, and when that mixes, you will have indigo.

3. The area where you are sitting becomes a revolving plate. Start rotating, and get the experience of turning around. Move around a few times, but not too fast. Start to breathe deeply; then stop rotating, and start again in the opposite direction. As you are turning, breathe deeply through your mouth, and take in all the indigo substance out of each of the six corners. Try to do this in one revolution.

4. As you stop revolving, hold in the substance, and let it

rise from the base of your spine all the way back up to your brow. Observe your reactions. Then begin turning back in the opposite direction, and blow the substance back into the six corners. Pause before you inhale again, observe what has happened to the substance and the room, and check any physical and psychological responses you may be experiencing.

5. Inhale and exhale a second time, just as before.

6. Now speed up your revolution, and inhale, following the same pattern as before, but this time more briskly. When you are ready to exhale, turn quickly in the opposite direction, and blow the substance upward, over the walls of the room and away.

FEEDBACK

This exercise is fairly straightforward. The only problem that usually crops up at first is difficulty in coordinating breathing and turning, which means that you may finish inhaling either before or after completing one revolution. Simple practice will help you regulate your breathing so that you reach all six points in exactly one breath.

The reason for the turning motion in this exercise is that I have discovered over the years how often the pituitary is clogged, which prevents its energy from circulating properly. Most people have no regulatory control over the pituitary at all. The revolutions are designed to loosen up our interior approaches to and from the pituitary and make its synthesizing functions more efficient. It is also important, at least when you begin the revolving, to let yourself be the axis for the motion. The axis may change during the exercise; the room may be moving instead of you or along with you. But you must be the axis at first so that the decision to revolve is your conscious act. Only your own activity can awaken the unconscious decisions lying within each chakra.

CROWN CHAKRA (PINEAL BODY)

THE SYMBOL

Crown

The symbol for the crown chakra is the lotus; the color is the rich purple of an orchid. For this exercise, your head becomes the calix, the bulb at the base of the lotus; the purple flower is floating above your head. Your neck and the rest of your body form the stem. The earth on which you are standing and which surrounds the stem of the lotus is the decaying bulb. When a lotus flower flourishes, its bulb decays, until the peak of the flowering is matched by the collapse of the bulb. But by this time a new bulb has begun to grow.

We can see the same cycle of growth and decay in the earth itself. At the close of each day, the sunset gives the world its final flowering. More fundamentally, the world never appears the same today as it did yesterday. Each morning is in a sense a rebirth, the beginning of the world, and you and each evening are the end, a death experience.

We have something to do with this cycle, too. If we and the world hinged onto us can develop holistically, becoming aware of earth evolution through self-evolving, then we will grow daily into advanced stages of existence more easily and with fewer problems. As this happens, we will be able to leave behind old developments without regret, thereby clearing the way for each new level of consciousness. We are the ones who are changing the earth. Our individual growth in consciousness means that we are efficiently and thoroughly transmuting all the energy that we are taking in and fully expressing it, holding nothing back.

This process ensures an intimate, transpersonal relationship to the cosmos. We begin, if only a little bit at a time, to live like higher beings, taking in our nourishment in the form of subtle, fine energy and giving it all back, fully integrated, to the cosmos.

The lotus flower symbolizes this transpersonal relationship in which we absorb fine cosmic energies and reissue them into the world. The lotus flower, like a water lily, lives surrounded by water. This water represents the currents of pure energy that surround us as well. Like the lotus, we should bend with the current, without putting up resistance.

In each individual chakra exercise, we are working with the flow of energy from outside to within and back out once more. But especially in this final crown chakra, we have a sharply defined symbol of our energy environment in the water surrounding the lotus. In terms of consciousness-raising techniques, the water is the energy field of whiteness that we create around ourselves for health. Before beginning any of these exercises, then, it is appropriate to radiate an energy field of pure whiteness.

BREATHING

As always, inhale through your mouth. But because you are a flower this time, imagine that you are breathing in at the top of your head. Flowers are relaxed when their petals are folded in, and they are at work transforming energy when their petals are fully extended. As you inhale, the petals above your head will extend. Their orchid-colored substance descends through the stem (your spine) to the base and then into the earth below.

The inhaled energy reaches below the gonads, the root chakra; feel it going down your legs. Let the energized substance nourish all the stem cells, soaking all your insides. While you are holding in your breath, have the substance rise up the stem, which is you, settle momentarily in the middle of your forehead, and then leave through a small area of your skull above it that is part of the flower bud, not the stem. In exhaling, gently blow the orchid-colored substance (or whatever color it has become) into the atmosphere. On the third breath, twirl the substance as it descends and rises. This revolution gives it more speed and energy, and the final exhalation can be more brisk.

For the meditations on the four chakras above the heart chakra, the first two breaths have been gentler and more rhythmic than in the first three chakra exercises because the heart chakra is the point at which we began dealing with more subtle energies. At the solar plexus level and below, the sluggishness of the energy system requires that we try to break up the solidity by heavy breathing.

THE MEDITATION

1. After settling into a relaxed pose and practicing some deep abdominal or paradoxical breathing, relax your attention to breathing, shut your eyes, and imagine a lotus flower floating on the top of your head. You are surrounded by water, and the flower is resting on top of the water. Fill in the picture. Your head is the flower bud, the rest of your body is the stem, and at the bottom, your feet are rooted in the decaying bulb. The color of the lotus and the atmosphere above it is a rich purple, the color of an orchid.

2. Inhale gently, taking in a good dose of the orchid-colored substance from the atmosphere. Let it descend all the way down to the bulb, at foot level; feel it descending and nourishing the stem. As you hold in your breath, let the substance rise to the top of your head. When you exhale, it drifts back through the flower into the air.

3. Observe what has happened to the color of the substance, what the lotus petals have been doing as you inhale

and exhale, and what feelings you have experienced as the substance has nourished your body. Do you feel any mental exhilaration?

4. Inhale again, very gently now, and observe the petals opening up. Let the purple substance go all the way down to your feet and then float up to the top of your head. Now exhale, letting it pass out of the top of your head and beyond. The petals are closing now as you finish exhaling. Pause.

5. The third time, inhale with a twist, so that the substance twirls down the stem, picking up speed and energy. It will swirl around your feet and then rise, twisting like the stripes on a barber pole, and nourish all your cells and the crown of your head. Now exhale with a sigh, and let the substance fly out the top.

FEEDBACK

If the lotus color becomes brighter each time, the growing whiteness or silver gray will come all the way down the stem, rather than remaining on top in the petals. At the final exhalation, you may see all the petals blow away, and then you will see the heart of the flower. You may see yourself inside that heart, like a little baby. Others see themselves reborn, floating above the lotus flower.

The commonest color that may intervene here is gold, the color from the heart chakra. It is also possible that your lotus may wither and die, but like all dying, this will be only the preliminary stage to new growth.

After you have become familiar with each of the chakra exercises you will want to practice them in an unbroken sequence to gain maximum benefit from them. When you do a series of combined chakra exercises, you will feel more energized when you have finished. Your vision may improve, too, making things appear brighter when you open your eyes. And of course as your energy begins to flow more freely, you should begin to see whiteness at the end of each part of the exercise. The whiteness does not have to look like a movie screen. It can be a foggy, cloudy, pulsating white, or a pale gray. All these are healthy resolutions, too.

There will be many pulsating points around your body, especially at the base of your spine, which should be rather warm. In fact, by the end of the third chakra exercise, you may feel that the pulsating points are twirling around with the green substance as well.

As I have mentioned, you may feel some tension or clogging in your throat or chest or even your forehead. This may be partly the result of a pacing problem. Let me explain by an analogy. You are driving on the freeway at forty-five miles per hour, and the engine is running smoothly. If you suddenly put your foot on the gas pedal to accelerate rapidly, the carburetor cannot process the fuel quickly enough, and so the whole car will tremor, a gasp or shock of reverberation, until everything can catch up to the new pace. The same thing can happen to your organism, in which case it does no harm to take the exercises more slowly. This will mean, however, that you will have to be able to breathe more slowly and deeply. And that takes us back to the benefits of working on your breathing. Learn to hold your breath for a reasonably long period of time and to exhale slowly, passively willing yourself to overcome your body's wish to speed up the breathing cycle. Not only is relaxation the consequence of deep breathing; it can also help you attain new levels of breath control and extension.

MANDALA MEDITATION

Preparation

Assume the proper position, and practice some paradoxical

deep breaths, inhaling deeply and exhaling slowly. Shut your eyes, and return to normal breathing.

Symbol

Imagine a large, square, open conduit in front of your face. Fill it with a red-orange substance, and let the substance swirl around inside the conduit for a moment. Become aware of the vast depths of the conduit, and note how the substance moves around in it, going back farther than you can see.

Action

Now draw all the red orange into your body through the mouth. Inhale deeply, taking it all in, and move all the red orange through your mouth and down to the base of your spine. Hold it there. Check your body and surroundings, the square, the substance, their color and shape, and your own feelings. Exhale slowly, and push all the red orange back inside the square conduit. Observe the colors now. For the second breath, follow the same pattern as before.

Resolution

The third time, inhale as before; but when you exhale, instead of blowing the substance inside, blast it around the outside of the square. Return to normal breathing, and observe. What color is the substance now? Is there any inside the box? How much is white? What are your own feelings? Is any part of your body sending out signals?

Symbol

Envision a transparent pyramid as big as you are, move inside it, and sit down. Now fill the pyramid with a pink substance or light.

Action

Use your mouth to suck in all the pink from every corner of the pyramid, just as if you were a vacuum cleaner. Let it flow down to the base of your spine; then let it drift up to the level of your spleen, at the top of your hips. Hold it, and observe. Exhale slowly, pushing the pink back into all the corners of the pyramid. For the second breath, follow the same pattern as before. Observe the pyramid constantly, noting any changes.

Resolution

The third time, inhale as before; but when you exhale, look upward, and blow the pink substance right out of the pyramid through an opening at the top. Return to normal breathing, and observe whatever is happening.

Symbol

Imagine that you are standing on a green circle. Think of the greenness as being very thick and stacked up around the edges of the circle, like a green sleeve with a coil inside it.

Action

Inhale deeply, and in your imagination, bend down, grasp the edges of the circle, and pull it up until it is level with the top of your head. Then bring it down close to you, as if you were tucking the sleeve inside itself. Feel the greenness gliding past the outside of your body. Stop it at your hip level, hold your breath, and during that pause, lift the cylindrical walls up to the midchest (solar plexus) level. Observe. Exhale, pushing the greenness of the wall up to the top of your head and over;

let it fall back down into the circle shape. Pause, and observe. For the second breath, follow the same pattern as before.

Resolution

The third time, set the cylinder spinning very quickly so that it starts to rise almost automatically with your hands guiding it up to your head, over, and down, right around your body. When it settles at midchest level, it will be swirling rapidly, like a whirlpool. Exhale forcefully, and push it up and away. Breathe normally, and observe.

Symbol

Imagine a transparent, hollow cross as big as you are, with four equal arms, the top and side arms being open-ended. Bring it close to you, and fill it full of sparkling golden-amber substance.

Action

Let a tube connect your mouth to the center of the cross, and inhale through it, drawing in all the yellowness and letting it sink to the base of your spine. Then, while holding your breath, let it rise up to armpit level. Observe everything. Exhale, and slowly force the substance back through the tube into the cross. For the second breath, follow the same pattern as before. Observe any changes taking place in you or the cross or the substance.

Resolution

The third time, inhale as before; but when you exhale, blow the substance forcefully out the three open ends of the cross so that it sprays out like a fountain. Breathe normally, but continue to observe.

Symbol

Visualize a large chalice before you. Fill it with a deep blue liquid, and then raise the cup to your lips.

Action

Slowly inhale, and as you do, drink from the chalice, savoring every swallow. Let the precious royal blue substance flow down your throat and into your body until it pools at the base of your spine. When the chalice is emptied, hold your breath and the liquid within you for a moment. Observe all feedback. Exhale, and let the liquid rise and flow back into the cup. Note all changes that may have occurred in the color and texture of the substance and any physical or emotional reactions that you may be experiencing. Inhale and exhale once more, repeating this visualization.

Resolution

With your third breath, forcefully inhale all the liquid in one gulp, pouring it down to the base of the spine. Pause. As you begin to exhale, lock your throat, and gag on the liquid as it rises. Maintain this locked position for a moment; then release the liquid and allow it to flow out. As it flows, both the chalice and liquid dissolve into nothingness. When the dissolution is complete, review your experiences by observing your total mental, physical, and emotional state.

Symbol

Imagine that you are sitting in the middle of a tall room

that has a star-shaped floor. The six corners of the star are filled with an indigo-colored substance.

Action

Inhale deeply, and notice that your body begins to spin in place. With each inhalation, you will turn a full circle (360 degrees). As you turn, breathe in all the indigo from the corners of the room. Let the substance settle at the base of your spine. As you pause before exhaling, your body stops turning, and you allow the indigo to rise up to the level of your brow. Remember to be fully aware of all feelings and sensations that you experience during this process. Exhale, allowing your body to spin in the reverse direction, and blow the indigo back into the corners of the room. Repeat this entire procedure with your next breath.

Resolution

On the third breath, inhale briskly and spin as before. When you exhale, turn quickly in the opposite direction, and blow the indigo out of the room, through the open roof above. Again, passively monitor all your reactions.

Symbol

 Your head is the calix of a lotus blossom whose purple petals extend above you. Your body is the stem that reaches through the water to the cool mud below. You are at rest, so the blossom is closed.

Action

Inhale, and feel the air entering through the top of your head. As you breathe in, the lotus petals extend, and the blossom opens. Your inhalation carries the orchid purple of the bloom down to the base of your spine. Even your legs begin to tingle with the nourishing energy you are absorbing. Hold in your breath, and allow the purple to rise up and settle for a moment in the center of your forehead. Exhale, and let the purple tinge the petals of the lotus with color. Notice the color of the lotus, and remember the feelings and sensations you experience. Inhale and exhale again in this same pattern.

Resolution

Inhale for the third time by breathing in and imagining that the air is swirling like a whirlpool into your body with ever greater intensity and speed. Let it swirl the purple color down the stem of your body. When this vortex of energy reaches your toes, it will reverse direction and spin upward. As it whirls out the top of your head, it may blow away the petals of the lotus and reveal to you the secret held inside the bloom.

When you have completed this sequence of visualizations, remain within the experiences you have had until the idea of awakening occurs to you. Carefully acknowledge and affirm all feelings, sensations, and insights that you have observed during the meditation. Then gently awaken to the world around you, feeling strengthened and fulfilled by your journey. Your body and mind will feel clarified, lightened, perhaps even tingling with energy for some time after awakening.

This delightful condition can be extended and experienced all the time, not just after meditation. When we can live our lives with this awareness, we have begun to discover our wealth of inner resources (one of the goals of meditating creatively that will be elaborated in Chapter 8).

8.

Harmony of Mind and Body

Mind and body are different expressions of the same thing: the unique part of the universe that is you. But we have come to think of the body as being the physical vehicle for the mind and of the mind as being the brain, which is the computer center for the complex muscular and neural structure that collects information about the world for us and reacts to that world. Aside from minor eccentricities, all brains and all bodies are the same. How, then, are we to account for the fact that we are all different?

Some scientists say our differences arise from the unique combinations of genetic heritage; social, cultural, and physical experiences; and instincts that form individual lives. Such a mechanical model seems to include everything except the most important quality of being human, that aspect that makes each of us unique: the ability to create, to envision what is not, and then to give it form in the world. We create every time we perceive connections between events, facts, or feelings that we never before noticed, every time we experience that flash of sudden understanding or find a new way to do something or make something beautiful. In fact we do very little that does not draw upon our creative capacity.

A machine cannot create; it can only mimic what it has been taught and react in predesignated ways. When we accept the idea that our bodies are machines whose functions are determined by external circumstances, we soon become "strangers in a strange land." Our bodies are separate from us, alien, and potentially threatening. No wonder we begin to block energy; no wonder we become attached to any situation that gives us temporary shelter from the awareness of our alienated condition. When we are attached to a situation or to the perpetuation of certain feelings or to the attainment of a specific goal, we are dominated by that attachment; our lives are no longer freely self-created but controlled by desire and fear.

Rather than seeing our bodies as separate entities, we need to perceive a relationship between mind and body. And for this relationship to be balanced, a fulcrum is needed on which the tension between mind and body can be balanced. That fulcrum is the soul, or spirit, the third aspect of the triune nature of the human being. The functional definition of this aspect is that it is the viewpoint from which we perceive the whole. It is the perspective we learn to attain when we become mediators in meditation, and it is the motivating and directing purpose of our existence. Mind and body are the worlds in which we can experience, learn, and manifest our creative potentials and understand ourselves to be cocreators of this universe. When we become conscious of this purposive part of our beings, we become aware of our souls, of the spirit within us. Opposites, such as mind and body, can then be seen as two sides of the same coin. All parts of creation are interconnected. We fail to perceive the whole when we become identified with any single aspect of it, as we do when we identify ourselves only with our cognitive, rational minds.

In order to become conscious again, we must disidentify from what dominates us. All the techniques of creative meditation can help us become aware of our attachments and thus cultivate a state of nonattachment. How do we disidentify? We raise our sights and take aim at our higher purpose, the reason for being that we perceive when we act as mediators in our lives. Paradoxically, we must attach ourselves to another goal in order to free ourselves from our present restricting attachments.

When we are born, we are attached to our mothers, and being attached is a fundamental aspect of living. Growing beyond our attachments is like climbing a mountain. Before releasing our hold on one footing, we must grasp the next step. In other words, we must see what lies ahead and be willing to move toward it, leaving our present level behind. This process is never completed. As we grow or climb higher, we envision expanded vistas and perceive fuller goals. We constantly become reattached and dominated, so we must continuously strive to set ourselves free. It is best to accept this as part of the cycle of living, with the consolation that every time we move beyond an attachment, we become more conscious and less vulnerable to rigidity and disease.

Attachment and energy stagnation are the primary sources of disease. They signal that we are no longer exercising our creative abilities. We forget about creative living as we fall into the illusion of a determined, mechanical world. We begin to inhabit our bodies as if they were something outside ourselves. This attitude leads to a duality in which mind and body are at war, and we are the victims.

When we become attached and rigid, we can become diseased. I believe that all diseases result from a lack of cohesiveness and harmony among mind, body, and spirit and therefore a lack of consciousness. As soon as you alienate yourself from your body or neglect a potential creative impulse, you suffer a loss of consciousness. The cumulative effect of many such suppressions is disease.

As a society, we are beginning to discover the inherent involvement of mind with body and to apply this insight to one of our major health problems: stress-related disorders. Psychosomatic medicine, the medicine of the future, provides a holistic perspective on the function of disease and health in the evolution of the individual.

Stress-related disorders occur when a person converts his or her anxiety into a physiological dysfunction; that is, a mental or emotional imbalance is transferred to the physical plane. This transference usually comes about because we refuse to recognize or deal with the emotional imbalance. The body is then forced to do the work, for anxiety does not go away just because we pretend it is not there. All of us have the capacity for dealing with our anxieties, and once we are aware of them, we become responsible for taking them in hand. Too often, though, it seems easier not to face them at all than to accept the challenge of growth.

Anxiety is different from simple fear. Whereas fear is a recognition of a real danger, anxiety is a looming sense, a vast cloud of uncertain, threatening possibilities. Once a fear is identified, it can usually be dispelled; but anxiety is harder to define and combat, often because its origin is not in anything specific. For the most part anxieties arise as a result of expectations. We are afraid that we cannot perform up to standard. Whose standard? Usually we try to live up to the standards of others, rather than to our own. Because we are ignorant about ourselves, we accept other people's expectations of what we are supposed to be and do. This means that we have to rely on others to validate our lives; we are directed by external demands rather than by inner vision. All this can be reversed when we take time to learn about ourselves and our own values.

The central issues in neurosis are the pain of chronic anxiety and what we do to avoid this pain. All psychiatric disturbances are the abnormal channels used by the organism to deal with this pain. An abnormal channel is the conversion of anxiety into physiological and psychological imbalance, which is at first self-perpetuating. Then the abnormality wears down the organism, and we become self-destructive.

Our bodies suffer many symptoms that are actually the result of reactions to anxiety. For example, there are dysfunctions of sensory and motor faculties such as stuttering. The stutterer gives orders to his motor faculty to speak, but it malfunctions. Many cases of blindness and deafness have the same cause. Anxiety may be entering our perception through a particular organ, perhaps the eye or the ear, and so we learn—to our detriment—to shut it out. Numbness in the face or the extremities is often caused by suppressed anxiety. Less serious symptoms are the familiar feeling of having a lump in your throat, perhaps to the point where you may have difficulty swallowing; stiffness in the joints; muscle tension; and general aches and pains.

No matter what it may be called and no matter what its physical sources and manifestations, every disease has its origin in a lack of consciousness. Somehow we have lost awareness of an important aspect of ourselves—our emotional expressiveness, our physical flow of energy or need for nourishment, or our spiritual reason for being. If any of the three dynamics of consciousness is repressed, an imbalance results, and physiological and psychological dysfunctions begin. The most specific, direct, and unavoidable consequence of the lack of consciousness is cancer.

I see cancer present in every person in its first stage, the stage of latency. To get a feeling for what latency is, think about your own growth in self-awareness. All the growth that is possible for you to achieve already exists, latent or hidden in your organism. It may be hidden to your conscious mind, but it is always alive and active in the paraconscious. By staying in vital communication with your paraconscious, you will always know the direction in which you are growing. But if your growth potential remains latent through your refusal to acknowledge it and develop, it becomes stagnant. Stagnant energy becomes an obstruction that inhibits the flow of many of the other forms of energy in your organism. This inertia is sufficient to cause a condensation affecting your biochemical processes. The body chemistry begins to produce mutants rather than normal cells, and the latent cancer begins to manifest itself.

Every moment of our lives demands that we change because the world constantly changes. If we do not resist or repress awareness of change, we grow and remain healthy. Only when we freeze, when we try to stop the flow, does change result in dysfunction. Any energy, faculty, capability, or physical aspect of the body that is restrained and not used causes the body's chemistry to produce substances that are denser than normal. I believe that cancer is a four-stage process. Latency is the first stage, and this densification, which results in benign tumors, is the second.

Stages one and two can be used as feedback, warning us of stagnation and its potentially worse effects. Do not imagine that the ability to be self-monitoring is some new experience that you have to try very hard to achieve. You are getting feedback all the time but are simply not paying any attention to it. For example, while you are reading this page, something I am saying may irritate you, and you get a headache or an eye irritation or just feel a bit uncomfortable. Somewhere in your organism, my words are resonating, but you are not aware of it, so the reaction appears to be random. It is not. Whenever your heartbeat changes unexpectedly or you perspire for reasons other than the weather or physical exertion or a ringing starts in your ear, recognize these experiences to be feedback about your internal state. If you ignore this feedback, you have denied your own insight. Then your cells begin losing direction, become neglected, and start to stagnate.

Another critical conscious moment of choice is when you suddenly doubt yourself. Even though you may have been following your own direction admirably for years, you may find yourself suddenly following someone else's ideas, by comparing yourself with someone else. This is the first step toward alienating aspects of yourself. Once communication among the three aspects of your being breaks down, the internal war begins. When the early warning signals are ignored or dealt with by severe repressive reactions, cancer moves into the third stage, malignant tumors. Now the body has developed a plant for the reproduction of mutant cells, and other bodily functions begin to suffer a loss of nutrition and energy.

I feel that cancer is completely curable through its first three stages. You do not have to look outside yourself for the cure. You already have it, and you need only to learn how to apply it. That cure is consciousness. Discover the part of mind, body, or spirit that is falling asleep and needs to be aroused. You can learn to reconnect this part of yourself to the rest of your being. At the early stages this means taking advantage of the feedback your organism already gives you. At the very least, concentrate on your cerebral feedback, for the brain acts as interpreter for the energies in the paraconscious and the unconscious. An enlightened person cannot fall ill with cancer, no matter how many cancer cells are injected into his bloodstream. Full consciousness is total immunity from disease.

At this point, creative meditation and the chakra checks can provide the essential information you need in order to reverse the degenerative process. The effects can be startling when you have the key and earnestly use it to redirect the energy, unblock the restraints, and evaporate the stagnation. In my own counseling experiences, I have seen people with severe symptoms of cancer achieve a total remission in a matter of weeks. Once the cancer has reached the fourth stage, however, and a high level of malignancy has developed, the entire system is often severely depleted. Although it is still possible to reverse the cancer, the body is already so exhausted that it has no strength to impart to the growth of healthy new cells. In such a case massive outside assistance is required, including biofeedback, relaxation exercises, psychotherapy, etc.

The difficulty of regenerating the diseased mind-body should encourage us to try actively to prevent the disease in the first place. Psychosomatic medicine emphasizes prevention. All the techniques suggested in this book for creative meditation provide clear and concise self-monitored information about your internal condition, as well as helping to prevent the stagnation of energy.

In order to be effective in these practices for the prevention of disease, we need to perceive that all parts of the world are interrelated. From this perspective we cease to be concerned with the processes of continual flux and interchange of energy. Nothing is lost or gained forever. All forms and all experiences appear, disappear, and recur again. That is the nature of energy.

When we begin to think of ourselves as energy, it is easier to appreciate the extent to which we must be interrelating with everything that exists. Energy cannot be destroyed. It can be transformed, but the sum total of universal energy remains undiminished. Every particle, every mineral that you find on the earth can be found within the human body. Every kind of energy in the earth's vegetable and animal kingdoms exists within the human organism in a form appropriate to human identity.

As humans, we have the capacity for self-transformation,

but only after we have realized our relationship to other forms of life. Even if you choose to ignore your relationship to the earth's array of energy forms, you will still be affected by them. You cannot stop the pattern of transformation of mass to energy to mass that is the universe.

Even when you become conscious of the energy around you and learn to alter, interrupt, or deflect it, you cannot destroy or create it. You can, however, destroy and create matter. All change involves destroying one form and creating another. There is no way to create without destroying or to destroy without creating. Remember that the words *create* and *destroy* are not automatically positive and negative. What if I create an ulcer in my body and at the same time destroy healthy tissue in order to create the diseased tissue? Would you find that a positive development? It is, in fact, the healing process in reverse.

Destruction and creation are going on all the time in an organism. Just as it takes two electrodes, a positive and a negative, to create an electric current, it takes both positive and negative elements to initiate a discharge of energy. Every particle in an organism has its positive and negative attributes, and when the organism is healthy, the two are in balance.

This is where awareness or consciousness can affect the interaction. When we know what we are creating and destroying and why, we have a better chance of achieving progressive development. Nothing is innately positive or negative. We are affected one way or the other according to what we want or think we want. For example, if you numb yourself in order to avoid feeling pain or a frightening emotion, is the relief of discomfort a positive or negative thing? I would consider that relief negative because it was obtained by blocking off part of your experience and thereby freezing the flow of energy.

Health can be defined as a condition in which an organism's energy patterns or rhythms are regulated and thus able to flow freely. There are also conditions of existence that far surpass anything that we call good health. Once we reach the healthful state created by consciously regulating the flow of energy, we can gain access to the vast potentials of physical existence. For example, if our energy centers, or chakras, were ever to operate at their full capacity, we would no longer have any need for physical food, and we would start to evolve into more advanced organisms. How is this possible? Fully functioning chakras are able to generate the necessary chemicals that are required by the organism for growth.

If no sluggishness or density were detracting from the operations of body and mind, all activity would occur at high vibratory levels. Therefore the nutrients required by the body could also be subtle in form, so subtle, in fact, that they could be generated from incoming photons or light. A body that attained a state of harmony beyond what we think of as mere health would transform light into electric energy in the chakras. A second transformation would then occur to turn the electric energy into the chemical form that nourishes the cells. To complete the circuit, the chemicals would turn back into electric energy that would be emitted by the chakras. Instead of getting energy from secondary sources, such as animals and plants, a person in total harmony would derive it directly from the sun, as plants do in photosynthesis.

Sleeping patterns would also change. Most people sleep many hours each night, but many still feel exhausted on awakening. That is because they have not really been at rest. The anxieties, chemical imbalances, and suppressed emotions that keep them in ill health affect them even more during sleep. If the issues that are frozen or feared are faced in creative meditations, they can be sufficiently resolved to prevent them from disturbing your rest. If you go to bed with a full stomach, your body must work to digest the food while you sleep, so you toss and turn and feel uncomfortable. Similarly, if your mind is filled with undigested material—worries, blocked insights, fears—you will suffer an equally restless night. I meditate before sleep in order to set my mind at rest. In this way my body can really absorb the benefits of its rest period, and I awaken refreshed after sleeping only a few hours each night.

In fact, I do not limit my meditation to any specific time of day. I use it as soon as a problem arises. Then I can contact the paraconscious mind and benefit from its resources of intuition and insight. In the passive stage of the creative meditation process, I can look at the situation objectively and then put the problem aside in order to let the solution appear. Whenever I energize a problem by allowing a flow of insight to interact with it, I know that the solution I find will not be laden with punitive and reactive judgments. We must become nonattached to our problems if we are to move beyond them and resolve them.

In Chapter 1 I described a few of the more sensational abilities that can be manifested when we become conscious of all the functions of our bodies and minds, not just the rational and voluntary ones. I have learned to be aware of the interdynamics of mind and body to the extent that I can control the flow of blood or demonstrate specific brain wave patterns when I choose. You have these potential abilities within you right now, and if you have practiced the exercises in this book, you probably have begun to experience them.

The primary personal benefits of creative meditation are: learning to regulate involuntary functions so that you can experience better health, resolving problems with greater creativity, and maintaining a perspective that allows you to understand your life and find peace of mind. But there are more effects than these. If I have a healthy body and an unfettered, active mind, and if I am aware of where my energy originates and how it operates, I will enjoy life more. I will also be more of a joy to others because they will see that this is possible. When we perceive only the negative sides of life and are bound by our fears and desires, we become competitive with one another. This is a type of personal alienation that many people in the world suffer. But if I share what I am with you, then I do not need to compete with you. This sharing is the opposite of narcissism, and it represents a flow of energy that is just as healthful for society as it is for personal being.

There is, after all, no need to prove one's own worth by negating someone else. We are all equal because each of us is essential to the other's existence. Each person plays a unique and perfect part in the scheme of the universe. When we understand this, we begin to understand the meaning of equality. We also experience the kind of universal love that embraces all the variations of expression that make up our world, rather than choosing certain parts to love and rejecting others.

I have suggested that our health is a barometer of our awareness of all aspects of our beings. Through creative self-analysis, we can learn to regulate ourselves and attain inner harmony. However as we achieve this heightened consciousness, we also take on an additional responsibility. I put it this way: As long as I am in this world, I have to serve the world in order to serve myself. And I see "myself" as being humanity, not just the individual "I am." Our duty, then, is to fulfill ourselves for the sake of all selves, as a body-mind-spirit unity, to express consciously one aspect of the universe.

NOTE

Jack Schwarz plans to establish in Gold Hill, Oregon, a spiritual, psycho-physical therapeutic complex where human beings can develop to the extent of optimal, spiritual, psychological, and physical health—wholeness. Such a place will be like a "medicine wheel," with many spokes to provide a multidimensional, all-inclusive, diagnostic, therapeutic training center existing and working in a broad framework of holistic methods, alternative methods of healing, preventive methods, and maintenance of optimal health adapted from many other cultural traditions as well as our own already available sources.

For further information, please contact:
Aletheia Psycho-Physical Foundation
515 N.E. 8th Street
Grants Pass, Oregon 97526

DUTTON PAPERBACKS OF RELATED INTEREST

Philosophy and Religion:

THE MIND OF LIGHT, Sri Aurobindo
ABOUT BATESON, John Brockman, editor
BEYOND THE GODS, John Blofeld
I-CHING: THE BOOK OF CHANGE, John Blofeld
THE SECRET AND SUBLIME: TAOIST MYSTERIES AND MAGIC, John
    Blofeld
THE TANTRIC MYSTICISM OF TIBET: A PRACTICAL GUIDE, John
    Blofeld
AMONG THE DERVISHES, O. M. Burke
ANOTHER WAY OF LAUGHTER, Massud Farzan
THE TALE OF THE REED PIPE, Massud Farzan
TRANSCENDENTAL MEDITATION, Jack Forem
VARIETIES OF THE MEDITATIVE EXPERIENCE, Daniel Goleman
BEELZEBUB'S TALES TO HIS GRANDSON (ALL AND EVERYTHING, *First
    Series*), G. I. Gurdjieff
MEETINGS WITH REMARKABLE MEN (ALL AND EVERYTHING, *Second
    Series*), G. I. Gurdjieff
VIEWS FROM THE REAL WORLD, G. I. Gurdjieff
THE AWAKENING OF KUNDALINI, Gopi Krishna
RADHAKRISHNAN, Robert McDermott, editor
LIFE AT ITS BEST, Meher Baba
A SENSE OF THE COSMOS, Jacob Needleman
THE NEW RELIGIONS, Jacob Needleman
THE BHAGAVAD GITA, Geoffrey Parrinder
ONLY ONE SKY, Bhagwan Shree Rajneesh
TEACHINGS OF RUMI, Jalaluddin Rumi
THE WALLED GARDEN OF TRUTH, Hakim Sanai
THE PATH OF ACTION, Jack Schwarz
THE SECRET GARDEN, Mahmud Shabistari
THE DERMIS PROBE, Idries Shah
THE EXPLOITS OF THE INCOMPARABLE MULLA NASRUDIN, Idries
    Shah
THE MAGIC MONASTERY, Idries Shah
ORIENTAL MAGIC, Idries Shah
THE PLEASANTRIES OF MULLA NASRUDIN, Idries Shah
THE SUBTLETIES OF THE INIMITABLE MULLA NASRUDIN, Idries Shah
TALES OF THE DERVISHES, Idries Shah
THE WAY OF THE SUFI, Idries Shah
WISDOM OF THE IDIOTS, Idries Shah
THE ELEPHANT IN THE DARK, Idries Shah and others
THE SPIRIT OF THE EAST, Ikbal Ali Shah
MYSTICISM, Evelyn Underhill
THE KAMA SUTRA, Vatsyayana
SUFI STUDIES: EAST AND WEST, Rushbrook Williams

The Mystic Sciences:

Psychology: